M000251749

WOMEN NAVIGATING

ADVERSITY

THE COURAGE THEY DIDN'T KNOW THEY HAD

SUE MACKEY

BOOK PUBLISHERS NETWORK

Book Publishers Network
P.O. Box 2256
Bothell • WA • 98041
Ph • 425-483-3040

Copyright © 2007 by The Mackey Group

All rights reserved. No part of this book may be reproduced, stored in, or introduced into a retrieval system, or transmitted in any form or by any means (electronic, mechanical, photocopying, recording or otherwise) without the prior written permission of the publisher.

10 9 8 7 6 5 4 3 2

Printed in the United States of America

LCCN 2007923951
ISBN 1-887542-50-7

Editor: Jenn Cassie
Cover: Laura Zugzda
Interior Layout: Stephanie Martindale

Contents

ACKNOWLEDGEMENTS

My profound gratitude to each woman profiled in this book. I am honored for having had the privilege of meeting each of you and am so thankful for your willingness to share your story in order that others may benefit. You touched my life, and I know you will touch many others as well through the courage with which you navigated your adversities.

To the untold number of friends, family members, and strangers who, when learning of my desire to write a book about women and their courage, enthusiastically and convincingly encouraged me to do it. Your faith that such a book would serve the greater good—including both men and women—was inspiring and motivated me throughout the writing process.

To Laura Tonkin, my business partner and long-time friend. This book would not have been possible without her constant support of this project, the sacrifices she made to make it a priority, and her critical eye for detail. Laura, your willing spirit and commitment to a friend will be a lifelong joy in my life.

To my editor, Jenn Cassie, for her discerning editorial eye and her ability to pull together a cohesive body of stories in just the right voice. Jenn, you've been a delight to work with. You've met every deadline and contributed an invaluable insight to every story. You have made me look good, and for that, I thank you.

To our layout designer, Stephanie Martindale, I offer many thanks for your dedication, professionalism, and friendship on this project as well as many others. Your delightful and much-appreciated sense of humor and good spirit make working with you a joy.

To my cover designer, Laura Zugzda, for her steadfast patience, once again, in working with me to capture the essence and meaning of the book through art. You are always a delight to work with in exploring design possibilities and a valued friend.

Disclaimer: The author acknowledges that some of the profiles contained within this book were not vetted or verified for their authenticity. However, most were read by persons knowing each particular story, who confirmed the story's accuracy as depicted by the author. The publisher and author are not responsible for any inaccuracies or misinformation presented as fact during the interviews. In two or more instances that have been noted as such, names have been changed by request in order to protect the privacy of children, family, or friends.

INTRODUCTION

Women Navigating Adversity: The Courage They Didn't Know They Had is a book about twelve everyday women from all walks of life who have persevered through incredibly difficult and often seemingly insurmountable challenges. Their stories will share what happened to them and describe how they navigated their way through, under, over, or around their onerous circumstances. Bad times happen to all of us, but how we manage our adversities determines the quality of our lives.

As you will discover, the remarkable women and their experiences described in this book reveal the power of faith and of quality relationships. Some of them had strong faith cemented during their childhood; others looked to a higher power later in life for guidance. For some, their relationships were lifelong, while for others they were fleeting. Nevertheless, without either faith or relationships, these women would never be where they are today. They could not have navigated their adversities, and they would never have discovered the courage they held within them.

These women experienced the same emotions and thoughts that you or I might have, if these adversities had intruded upon us when we least expected it. They have had times of despair, desperation, loss, doubt, fear, and hopelessness. Many have experienced guilt, shame, embarrassment, and relentless criticism and pessimism from family and friends. There were times when thinking positively, while being bombarded with negative events and feelings, was impossible, just like it is for so many of us. Thinking negatively was the easy way out.

The difference inherent in these twelve women is that they refused to remain trapped by their circumstances and negative emotions. Events may have caused them to be labeled "victims," but they refused to wallow in self-pity. They had no formal training in courage. They didn't attend survival and coping classes, like they do in the military. Instead, their courage grew organically as they successfully navigated through each obstacle in their path. Their self-esteem increased as they acquired new skills and perfected existing skills. Nothing came easily, but every day—whether it held failure or success—they learned from each small victory and each defeat. They took responsibility for their decisions and actions, both good and bad, and knew that whatever fruit they would be blessed with would have to be earned.

This book has been written for you. While these women are inspirations to us all, my book is a success only if you discover that you have the ability to overcome adversities and succeed. There is no magic to it. Take something from each of these stories and use it to write a better story for yourself. And after you do, promise me you'll share it by writing or e-mailing. These women have given of themselves and revealed a lot in order to give you hope, purpose, and faith that when life deals you a bad hand, you will find the strength and the conviction to navigate through it successfully.

CHAPTER ONE

LAURA

MEET LAURA TONKIN. Today she is a highly esteemed consultant and writer, hailed internationally for her subject-matter expertise. But only a few short years before she earned that distinction, she was living a life filled with drugs and heavy partying and was futilely searching for love and connection to fill a gaping hole that a childhood trauma had left. Where did she find the strength and the courage to make such a radical change for the better? The same place she found fortitude and bravery her whole life: inside herself.

Laura was born, raised, and has lived most of her life in the greater Seattle area. The eldest of three children, she knew nothing but bliss until her thirteenth year. She and her brother and sister lived in middle-class suburbia, had two full-time working parents, and grandparents nearby to visit every Sunday for dinner. Childhood couldn't have been better; Mom and Dad never fought, and the kids were loved.

But life isn't always as perfect as it might appear. Their parents' marriage was not the ideal one it had seemed, and they unexpectedly announced their divorce. To compound the children's disbelief, their mother announced she was moving with them to Montana (two years later, their father left Washington for California, adding even more instability to their lives). They were being uprooted from the security and safety of the only home they'd ever known, the school pals they grew up with, and those special Sunday dinners with their grandparents. How could this be? Laura's young mind begged to know. Her folks never fought like their friends' parents did. So how could a happy, secure, and loving home come to such an abrupt end, leaving three children confused and upset with no acceptable explanation? The answer, Laura would later learn, was the immaturity and insecurities of both of her parents, as well as the use of alcohol to avoid dealing with the problems at hand rather than facing them head-on. What was immediately clear was that the kids' lives had changed forever and they were going to have to grow up fast. The lessons learned and skills acquired were not those meant for young kids to be burdened with.

At thirteen, Laura was no longer a spirited, happy young teenager. She was put in charge of her nine-year-old sister and eleven-year-old brother while her mother worked. Dad was no longer home from work to tend to their needs or listen to them tell of their days at school. Neither were the neighborhood mothers around to look after them when Mom and Dad were late getting home. Their mother worked late, seldom made it home for dinner, and was too tired when she did get home to fully participate in their lives. Not only did the location of their home change, but everything about their lives took a dramatic turn, much for the worse.

Instead of maintaining high grades in school as she had until the divorce, Laura's new responsibility of caring for her siblings took precedence over her schoolwork. Her grades quickly plummeted. It didn't take long for her to realize that filling a mother's shoes at thirteen with two distraught and confused siblings was no easy task. But she took a deep breath and learned to do the best she could, including supporting her siblings through their growing emotional needs. With no preparation and minimal understanding, she managed to juggle her responsibilities.

But as the months rolled on, Laura's need for emotional support and time to spend with friends grew. What she really ached for was her family to be back together again and life to return to how it should be—like the carefree, happy days before the divorce. Most of all, she longed for her father and the love that he so freely showered her with each day before they left Seattle.

Unable to have her father's presence, she did the next best thing in her eyes: she started hanging out with the older boys in school. With her vivacious personality and her blonde, tall, pretty looks, she either dated them or acted the part of their kid sister. The boys considered her one of their best friends, and it was this group that introduced Laura to alcohol and speed. Friends, alcohol, and drugs filled the void caused by the loss of her mother in a sense, her father, the neighborhood and school friends she'd left behind, the separation from her grandparents, and the vanishing of her childhood innocence. She was on a downhill slide with no brakes.

Soon, the reality that her mother couldn't provide financially for three growing children set in, and Laura began taking on part-time jobs for lunch money and to pay for what were now considered extras. The burdens quickly grew too heavy. Between being there for her brother and sister, working, school, dating, and partying, she was quickly overwhelmed. Something had to be eliminated off her plate. She couldn't abandon her brother and sister, and she needed her job in order to help her mother. Her time with friends was crucial for her emotional satisfaction. Fed up with her suffering schoolwork and classroom absences, the school principal gave her an ultimatum: either she could quit school and retain her earned credits, or she would be kicked out and lose them all. So her young, directionless, and overburdened mind chose to quit school.

Now, at seventeen, Laura was a high school dropout. Just four years earlier, she was an exemplary student at the top of her class, with a future ahead of her filled with academic accolades and college scholarships. But that was before the divorce, when education was a family value. After the divorce, Laura's life revolved around coping with losses and burdens she was unprepared for. Her future went from high expectations and opportunities aplenty to a bleak one filled with partying, working without a diploma, and looking for love and acceptance in all the wrong places. Her focus had shifted from family values to survival mode. What she didn't know was that the lessons she would learn and the skills she would acquire, when directed and used appropriately, would serve her well in time. But for now, she was headed down the destructive path of a teenager out of control.

After three years of life in Montana, Laura's mother decided to move her family back to the Seattle area. Within a year of the move, Laura got married. At just eighteen years old, she made a decision she would quickly regret. He wasn't a husband—he was a tyrant, and a jealous, abusive one at that. He owned Laura, and he let her know it. She was not free to come and go; she was living as if in a prison. In perpetual fear of her husband's terrifying behavior and with encouragement from her mother, she managed to run away in the middle of the night with the clothes on her back, her dog, and $350. She filed for divorce and was emancipated from her terrible marriage by their second-year anniversary. Two years of torment and imprisonment was behind her. He was not the man she was searching for; he was not her father.

Still searching for a father figure to fill that void, Laura married again almost three years after her first divorce. That marriage lasted a year before she bolted. Drugs and alcohol became a more active part of her second marriage. There was no physical abuse this time, but she still hadn't found what she was looking for. She was a young woman searching to recover what she'd lost and hoping her unsuspecting new husband would make up for all that she longed for. It was an impossible task to accomplish. Life in the fast lane continued. But unbeknownst to her, Laura's life was about to change dramatically.

What Laura did have going for her was an admirable work ethic. She was taught this during her early years when her family was still together, and she'd had it reinforced during the years following her parents' divorce. Those years spent in Montana raising siblings and working a job hadn't been for nothing. She had learned much and had acquired invaluable life skills she would learn to use to her advantage later in her still-young life.

Marriage, she was beginning to realize, did not provide a solution to her sense of aloneness, nor did it fill the fatherless hole she felt in her heart. Expecting someone else to make the pain go away would not give her the security she was searching for. Instead, she decided to focus her attention on doing something productive with her G.E.D., which she had earned shortly after returning to Seattle, and her certification from a community college as an aesthetician, specifically a nail artist. From the moment she began doing nails, she realized she excelled in her craft and, more importantly, in her relations with her clients. Her personality and ability to listen intently were magnetic to her customers. In a few short months, she had more business than she could handle and more referrals than any of her colleagues. Realizing she had the ability to attract and retain customers, her dream of owning her own salon formed. She realized that if she provided a quality service and appreciated her customers, success would follow.

But first, she had to find money. She had practically none, but she did have some Alaskan crab fishermen friends who made substantial profits from their trade. The very first one she approached agreed to finance her dream. They made a deal: he'd put up the money and she'd manage the business. Within months, a salon, Exposè, in Sammamish, Washington, was built, and Laura was in business. Although Laura and her business partner didn't know it, she was now managing one of the riskiest business start-ups. Most salons will fail, just ask any banker. Marketing, good help, and smart management are typically not the hallmarks of a salon entrepreneur's skill set. Emotions, not sound business logic, often drive many of their business decisions. Management and staff frequently resent their clients or are too absorbed in themselves to really care about their customers and their needs. But Laura, with her energetic and vivacious personality and her street smarts gained from working customer service jobs, knew exactly what customers wanted, and she enthusiastically gave it to them. The more good will she gave to her customers, the more good will they gave in return, including gifts, large tips, and friendship. Her first year-end financials revealed that she and her staff had generated $250,000 in sales. Needless to say, it was a highly impressive result for a young twenty-four-year old with no formal business training.

While many new business owners allow pride to cloud their good sense, Laura was not one of them. She knew what she didn't know. Aware that she didn't have the skills to sustain or increase revenues or the knowledge of how to manage employees effectively, she sought outside help. Her partner, a fisherman, didn't have the skills either and was for all intents and purposes an absentee partner, fishing off Alaska for months at a time. She wanted to succeed and was willing to do whatever it took to make that happen. She began looking for someone to help her achieve continued growth.

She asked a simple favor of a stranger: Can you help me? Would you teach me how to manage and grow my business? That person happened to be me. After talking with her, I observed a twenty-six-year-old woman who was hungry for knowledge and new skills, willing to listen and act, had no pity party going for a childhood fraught with despair and loss (victim was not in her vocabulary), and wanted to learn how to manage her fears. I agreed unequivocally to help her.

With the first year behind her and having built her quarter-million-dollar business in a small suburban community, we set the salon on course to solidify the existing business and stretch for $300,000 in revenue by the end of her second year. We achieved that milestone and met to discuss what the future would be for the business. Decisions had to be made for increased success. We chose to grow by acquiring a larger space. This would require either expanding the existing location or moving the business into larger accommodations. Wisdom dictated a more cost-effective move to a larger location. And as luck would have it, a new shopping center within walking distance, with a grocery store as the anchor tenant, had space available. After negotiating a deal with the management company for space, and prior to Laura signing a ten-year lease, we had a meeting of the minds. A commitment had to be made by Laura. The new location would be more expensive, and a term of ten years couldn't be taken lightly. In addition, she would have a very different landlord than the two friends she had now in her existing location. These people would be all business. An hour was spent looking at the new space and discussing Laura's future and what she wanted from it. Finally, she turned with tears in her eyes and told me something unexpected. She said that she couldn't picture spending ten more years in the salon business. She wanted out. "What will you do?" I asked. She replied, "I'd like to work with you." She wanted to leave the salon and learn the business of consulting.

This seemed a gutsy statement considering it was coming from a high school dropout, an aesthetician, and a young woman who hung out with a rough crowd of drug users. I was speechless. I could not come up with an adequate response. How, I pondered, would I tell her that it wouldn't work? Instead of telling her that right away, I told her instead that I'd think about it and let her know.

As I thought the situation through, I began to soften a bit toward the idea of giving Laura a shot. I couldn't readily figure out what she would be qualified to do, though. She did have some very desirable skills that would compensate for her lack of knowledge. But how, I thought, would she apply them in the business that I do? Also, major changes would have to occur. Would she be willing? There was something inside of her—a spark and a willingness—that told me she would do whatever it took to add value. Taking a chance on her was not a bad decision, provided she was willing to agree to my conditions.

I made a deal with her. She had little knowledge of what I did, but she had a host of skills, none of which were learned in the academic environment but all of which were vital to success, with or without an education. We agreed these skills would become beneficial once she acquired the technical skills she needed. I told her she should maintain her nail business for the time being and leave room in her schedule to shadow me and absorb as much as she could as quickly as possible. In addition, we agreed that she would only get compensated once she came to me and demonstrated that she could contribute to the business. Believing she was entitled to nothing unless she earned it, she readily accepted.

Another stipulation of mine was that she had to ditch her hard-partying lifestyle, which included her partying friends. The excessive drinking and drugs would have to go. She'd have to agree to buy some appropriate business attire. The beauty salon outfits—miniskirts, four-inch heels, provocative clothing—just wouldn't work. As I explained, I've worked hard for my business and my reputation; I was not willing to have it put at risk by her behavior on or off the job. If she complied with all of those things, I was willing to give her a chance. Failure to do any one of the things I asked of her meant the agreement was off. No second chances would be offered, and no excuses would be tolerated. She agreed to honor each one, and something told me she would keep her commitment to me. I knew it would be incredibly difficult for her. After all, she'd have to abandon all that was familiar to her, leaving behind her comfort zone of friends and lifestyle for the second time in her life.

Within a month, a buyer for the salon was found, and its ensuing sale was complete. There was no turning back now. Laura walked away from her friends, and the partying and drugs consequently stopped. She had new clothes and a new look. She was committed, excited, and very much afraid. Because of her past experiences, trusting me was a huge obstacle for her that she struggled with constantly. But her worry was for naught. I, too, honored my commitment to her as she had to me.

Within six months, Laura came back to me. She informed me that she had acquired enough knowledge and had the required technical skills now to work on some aspects of consulting projects. She wanted to charge for her services, and I agreed. I had known two months earlier that she should be compensated now, but we had a deal. She had to come to me and tell me that she deserved compensation. This was important to her self-esteem and to her future. I knew it was hard for her to do; it took guts, but she needed to experience asking for what she had earned. It was a hugely effective tool in building her confidence.

Within three years, Laura was well on her way to gaining recognition for her work. She had found her niche and was perfecting it. She became highly skilled in developing skill and performance standards for any occupation or process. Today, Laura is known internationally for the work she does. It is not uncommon to find her surrounded by PhD's or traveling across the country to participate in meetings as a subject-matter expert. Who could have foreseen that exceptionally well-educated people would seek advice and assistance from a high school dropout with only a G.E.D.? But Laura was motivated to acquire knowledge and to become the best at what she chose to do. Her street smarts coupled with her desire have driven her to the top of her chosen expertise.

During the last two years, Laura has added "co-author" to her long list of accomplishments. To hear her parents' pride as they speak of their daughter will bring tears to your eyes.

Laura and her father have an extraordinary and very close relationship today. He has resumed an active role as her strongest, most ardent supporter. She's no longer searching for a father figure; she has him. He's always been there.

🌱 🌱 🌱

Author's Observations:

Laura's childhood, although laden with inappropriate responsibilities, equipped her with a wealth of knowledge and skills that, when applied to building her future, ended up serving her well. Instead of whining about what she'd gone through, she used the adversities to her benefit. Her courageous willingness to make tough choices and step out of her comfort zone paid off. Most importantly, Laura had the necessary self-confidence and self-awareness to realize that she deserved a far better life than the one she was previously allowing herself to live. She took a risk and put her trust in me—a stranger—in order to achieve a productive, successful, and healthy life.

CHAPTER TWO

ROBIN

MEET ROBIN PRESSNALL. She is a woman on a mission—a mission unlike many others. Robin is the founder and executive director of Small Paws Rescue, an internationally recognized Bichon Frise animal rescue organization, headquartered in Tulsa, Oklahoma. Although she specializes in rescuing the Bichon Frise breed, her rescue model is used across the world for all types of mixed and purebred dogs. Founded in June of 1998, Small Paws Rescue has in excess of 6,000 members in twenty countries subscribing to its newsletters and over 800 volunteers nationwide. But as is the case for many successful people, Robin's childhood stacked the odds against her for a noteworthy and meaningful life. Living in poverty with an abusive mother, her chances of escaping from under the thumb of exceptionally bad luck were minimal, according to statistics. Only someone with incredible strength and unwavering faith would have been able to climb up out of that shadow and accomplish something worthwhile in life. Robin Pressnall is just such a person.

Born in Oklahoma City in 1956, Robin was raised as an only child. Her father, a hardworking man with only an eighth-grade education, owned a lawn mower repair shop. At best, it provided enough income for the bare essentials and nothing more. Her mother, from Robin's earliest recollection, was extremely cruel and physically abusive to her daughter and husband. Although her dad tried his best to protect Robin, it wasn't always possible. Robin later learned that the next-door neighbors often heard what was happening inside of her home but due to social pressures and no legal requirement, they felt that it was not their business to intercede. A plethora of expensive prescriptions managed to ensure that her mother's drug supply was plentiful while her violence went unchecked and the family became financially drained. Her mother may have been drugged and pain-free, but her victim, Robin, endured a childhood of agony and fear… that is, until everything came to a head in Robin's senior year of high school. One too many emergency room visits ended a life of torment for this teenager. The hospital where Robin had been taken after her mother's final attack even posted a security guard outside of her room to protect her from her own mother. With the hospital's assistance, Robin was finally removed from her home and placed with another family within the community. Here, missing her daily interaction with her father but safe from her mother's violence, Robin finished high school.

In school, Robin loved her music class and loved to sing. Singing offered her peace and joy that she could store in her mind and heart and recall at a moment's notice—for instance, when she was home alone with her mother and needed it most. Literature was second on her list of favorite classes. When she read a book, she could wander to places far away from the torment of her mother. School became a safe haven, a respite from home. And it was there that she discovered her first angel. Joanne Carlson, Robin's vocal music teacher, saw beyond Robin's poverty and deprivation. The clothes Robin wore, the bruises she tried to hide, and the fear and sadness etched across her face when she wasn't playing music or singing did not deter Ms. Carlson from believing in Robin's potential for a bright future. Someone needed to nurture her and her talent, to guide her and open doors for her. Ms. Carlson decided she would be that person.

Unbeknownst to Robin, Ms. Carlson and several other caring and dedicated teachers took their cause to Oklahoma City University.

There they pleaded their case: they asked the college to grant a young girl with talent, heart, and a rough start in life a full four-year scholarship, including tuition and room and board. It wasn't until the scholarship was in place that Robin was called into the counselor's office during her senior year. Believing that she was being accused of doing something wrong, Robin went tearfully; she wasn't used to being called into the counselor's office. Surrounded by all of her teachers, Robin learned of their secret gift. Robin was speechless and crying tears not out of fear, as she was moments before, but out of disbelief and overwhelming gratitude. This was the kind of thing she'd read about but had never imagined would happen to her. The love that her mother wouldn't provide for her was atoned for in spades by a handful of Oklahoma City teachers.

Without hesitation, Robin today relays this message embedded in her soul: "You never know if you're going to be the teacher that makes a difference in a child's life. How many kids are falling through the cracks because the politically correct police will vilify them if they reach out, show a kid they care, and believe in them? I wouldn't be where I am today if teachers hadn't taken me under their wing. It sickens me when I think of how little teachers are paid. It's an American tragedy."

Robin left for Oklahoma City University, majoring in fine arts, living in the dorm at Walker Hall, and working a part-time job. Life was good. With a rough eighteen years behind her, she was now being exposed to another side of life, far away from deprivation and torment. She was introduced to a world of refinement, romance languages, privilege, and world-class entertainers. Music students were hosts and escorts, while also playing music for Oklahoma City's most elite. It was her university experience that changed Robin. She discovered the magic in observing and duplicating the good things she was experiencing and throwing away the bad times of the past.

But real life imposed itself onto Robin once again. Her dreams of a life as a singing star slipped away from her one fateful day in her twenty-first year. She was diagnosed with tumors on her vocal cords and was told that not only would singing again be forever out of the question, but she would also have to learn to talk again after surgery. All her dreams that she had hoped to achieve—a career on stage and a life of privilege—had vanished. Incredibly, Robin was able to speak immediately after her surgery. But according to the doctors, her singing career was still gone with no hope of return.

Her singing voice may have been lost, but her newly acquired sense of value and worth as a respectable young woman remained with her. She no longer felt like, or looked like, an abused, poor girl. She didn't have any money to burn, but she quickly learned that didn't mean she had to act or think that way. Upon her college graduation, Robin entered society as a confident, dignified, and accomplished young woman. And to everyone's astonishment, she slowly recovered her singing voice after months of vocal therapy. However, it was clear that she still wouldn't be able to pursue a stage career. So she decided to do the next best thing.

As one might expect, Robin chose to become a teacher. She wanted to give back what had been given to her. She wanted to lead young minds and hearts into the world with the gift of knowledge and be an angel to those in need of one. After all, several had entered her life at the right time and place, opening doors and shining lights to follow. "I wanted to influence just one child, to make a difference in his or her life like those who had for me," she explains. Robin began teaching ninth and tenth graders vocal lessons and music. She also met and married the man she thought she'd spend her life with. But soon after her teaching career and marriage began, they both came to an end. Unhappy in her marriage, Robin simultaneously realized that even though she loved influencing young people's lives for the better, teaching wasn't making her truly happy either. With her upbeat, bubbly personality and can-do attitude, she was encouraged to pursue a career in real estate.

Robin sold real estate for six years in Oklahoma City. But her thoughts about her failures—her abject childhood, her lost voice, her distant teaching career, her defeated marriage, and now her successful but personally unrewarding career selling real estate—constantly threatened to sink her into the murky underground of depression.

Lonely, sad, and confused about her life, Robin saved her real estate commissions and decided to travel to Europe to visit friends who had moved to Germany. Little did she know that her life was about to be changed in a way that she could never have imagined.

At JFK International Airport in New York, as Robin sat waiting to board the 747 bound for Frankfurt, she exchanged smiles with an attractive man in the gate area who she thought looked as if he were from "back home" in his blue jeans and cowboy boots. He was a consolingly familiar sight amid unfamiliar surroundings. With any luck, he'd be seated near her on the long nine-hour flight ahead, she thought. After boarding the plane, she went to the back in search of her seat, while the intriguing gentleman seated himself up front in business class.

Settled beside what appeared to be one of the only empty seats on the plane, her flight made its way across the Atlantic Ocean. Surrounded by clear skies above and a deep blue sea below, Robin drifted in and out of thoughts about her past, present, and future. Life wasn't turning out the way she'd planned. Her God-given gifts and talents were not being used to their fullest, and now that her real passion—singing—was out of the question, what was her destiny? And what, she wondered, were her other gifts and talents? Would there be something else in her life she could become as passionate about as music? What, she pondered while forty thousand feet above the earth, would her future bring? To interrupt her confusion, intermittent flashes of the man in the business section danced through her mind as she contemplated life hereafter. She wanted to talk with him and get a break from her loneliness. She'd prayed for an empty seat beside her for such a long trip, but now it seemed pointless as nobody was even sitting there. She'd have gladly given up the space for his companionship. But within an hour of the plane reaching cruising altitude, Robin looked up and saw the man heading down the aisle toward her. He asked her if the seat beside her was taken, and soon they were talking like old friends. Robin told the stranger about her childhood, her failed marriage, her love of animals, and her desire to have the kind of passionate life that she had only read about in novels or seen in movies. They talked for eight hours straight. She learned that his name was Dale and that he lived in Tulsa, only ninety minutes from her home in Oklahoma City.

The next morning when the plane was ready to land, the man returned to his seat for landing. As he left, an old woman seated near her whispered to Robin: "Keep this close to your heart. Love like this comes along once in a lifetime. Don't let it get away." Mystified, she assured the lady that she had just met this man and they had only shared a plane ride, nothing more. As Dale waited for Robin at the arrival gate, the enigmatic old woman reached him first and told him that he had just met the woman with whom he would spend the rest of his life. Dale and Robin both laughed at the charming lady, wondering if she had been reading too many romance novels.

Although Dale had given Robin his business card, she had infuriatingly misplaced it. Five months later, however, Robin's thoughts were still consumed with Dale. She even tried hypnosis to recall his last name to her, with no luck. Remembering that it started with "PR," she decided to go through the Tulsa phone book. Bingo. She found him and called him.

Robin soon learned that on the plane that day in January, she had indeed met the love of her life, Dale Pressnall. Filled with gratitude, Robin wanted to locate the little old woman who had told her not to let Dale get away and invite her to their upcoming wedding. But after an exhaustive search through their records, TWA confirmed that the seat where Robin had seen the old woman sitting had been empty— the only other empty seat on the flight, in fact. There had been no woman, elderly or otherwise, sitting in that spot. Robin believed that again an angel had guided her, this time to her future husband.

Dale, twelve years older than Robin, was a highly successful environmental engineer. For the first time in her life, Robin didn't have to work. She could pursue new interests while still searching for something she could be passionate about. Her new interests— decorating, shopping, and lunching with friends—provided momentary happiness, but never enough to fill the void she couldn't seem to satisfy. Her marriage was all she had hoped for, and her life was picture-perfect for a girl who had never before even visited the part of town in which she now lived. But after eleven years of mind-numbingly repetitive shopping trips and long lunches, Robin looked back, looked forward, and realized this was not how she wanted to spend the rest of her life. It was a good and envious life by many people's standards, but it didn't have any real substance, meaning, or importance to her.

Early on in her young life, Robin had made a conscious decision to remain childless. The fear that she'd turn out to be a parent like her mother, whether through genetics or through how she was raised, was inescapable. The safest course, she believed, was to leave parenting to those who hadn't experienced the wrath of an angry, vicious mother. But mothers have a purpose—a reason for being that is greater than themselves—that they embrace with unconditional love. With Robin's continued doubts about motherhood, she prayed for God to show her something else of substance that she could embrace, something larger than herself, something she could dive into and be passionate about. Robin wanted to leave something lasting and purposeful behind and give something back to the world. There had to be something she could do to make the world a better place.

As often happens, opportunities surface when least expected, and such was the case with Robin. Although heroic measures had been taken, Nicholas, her faithful canine companion of many years, died of cancer. With a gaping hole in her heart, it was suggested to Robin that she look for another dog to love and care for. Taking the advice, Robin decided on a Bichon Frise puppy. She and Dale made a trek to Missouri in search of a Bichon breeder they had seen advertised. Their directions led them to a dirt road leading up to the breeder's house. As soon as Robin laid eyes on the property, she began to question her judgment in making the trip. Alongside the driveway was a dead horse, which appeared to have been lying there for quite some time. Dale asked her if she wanted him to turn around, saying this might be one of those dog farms he'd seen featured on the news. Robin's answer was that if this was a bad place, then they absolutely had to go in and rescue the puppy they had seen in the ad—along with the puppy's mother, father, brothers, sisters, and any others they could liberate.

Tentatively, she and Dale went to the house and knocked. What they saw when the door opened repulsed them. The house was filthy, smelled like a sewage tank, and was filled, wall-to-wall, with puppies and dogs. The place was worse than a pigsty. She and Dale picked up the puppy they had seen in the ad, but the breeder refused to sell the dog's parents. Robin was nonetheless stirred to action. This experience was Robin's introduction to rescuing Bichons.

Robin returned to Tulsa determined to take action against the abuse of these dogs. She soon learned the specific term that is used within the vast network of dog rescuers for what she had seen: a puppy mill. Puppies are bred for income purposes only, with total disregard for the welfare of the animals or the outcome of the litters. It's reminiscent of factories a century ago with no labor laws…work 'em till they drop. It's much the same in puppy mills: work the mother dog until she's dead, and invest as little as possible in food and veterinary expenses. Horrified at what she was learning, Robin was committed to shutting this operation down and saving the dogs. Knowing nothing about dog breeding or commercial kennels, the computer was her best resource. But with no computer skills, Robin first had to learn how to operate it and search for information.

Within weeks of returning from Missouri, Robin was online learning all she could about dogs and rescuing them from owner and commercial breeder neglect. She had asked God to show her something she could wrap her mind and soul around, and He did: rescuing dogs, specifically Bichons, by the thousands. In June of 1998, with the help of twenty-five dog-loving volunteers, her "magnificent obsession" was up and running. Small Paws Rescue, a ministry born of people from all faiths, had finally given Robin the passion that she'd been searching for.

Their first miracle rose out of the ashes of wildfires skipping across Utah in 2000. Towns were burning, and people were ordered to evacuate. Many large animals were left behind, and other smaller animals like dogs and cats scrambled for a hideout. During the height of these wildfires Robin received a call from a fellow volunteer, Sherrill Street, pleading for help. The fire was engulfing Sherrill's town, and she had to leave immediately. She could get her dogs out, but not her goat and horse. Before Robin could respond to her plea, the phone went dead. Robin sent out urgent e-mail requests for prayers for the safety of Sherrill and her beloved animals. When Sherrill returned home, she saw that everything surrounding her house was charred, with the exception of a green patch of grass where Sherrill saw her hoofed family members grazing peacefully. Robin's Small Paws Rescue prayer chain had worked, just like it continues to today.

Having survived a painful childhood, many lost dreams, and a failed marriage, Robin is convinced she has gone through life surrounded by angels, from her teachers to the mysterious woman on the plane. When adversity struck, miraculous opportunities followed. Dale and Robin are still happily married and just celebrated their twenty-first wedding anniversary. Small Paws Rescue continues to grow, rescuing between 100 and 150 Bichons every month. She says that Small Paws Rescue is a greater blessing in her life than she ever knew was possible. The Small Paws Rescue prayer ministry continues today, in twenty countries around the world.

To sum up Robin's work with Small Paws, she believes that her organization isn't just about rescuing the dogs. "Small Paws is really about the people who adopt the dogs and about our awesome God who loves those people," says Robin. "I believe that God called me to get this message out to a hurting world: if God will take care of a homeless little dog, a little dog with a lifespan of only a few years, think of how much more God will take care of His human children and their families. When we step out in faith to help those in need, God provides the ways and the means to accomplish those purposes." Through her devoted faith and her confidence in her own eventual self-discovery, Robin was able to survive the hard curveballs life threw her way with dignity, hope, and courage, ending up with the fulfilling life she's always dreamed of.

🌾 🌾 🌾

Author's Observations:

When dreams are stolen by unpredictable events, most people give up—but Robin wasn't one of them. With her goal of being a singer destroyed, she could have easily lived her life with regret and resentment, but instead she searched for something else that she could wrap her arms around. Her prayers to find passion in her life were answered in a most unlikely way. But had Robin only prayed and not been open to chartering unknown territory, she'd still be decorating and lunching her days away. Her faith, her husband's unconditional love, and her volunteers' support kept Robin focused on what could be, not what should have been.

CHAPTER THREE

GWEN

MEET GWEN FRASER. By all appearances, Gwen's life seems to have been rather calm and uneventful. She exhibits the poise and the gentle spirit of an uncomplicated woman of faith surrounded by the love and support of her family and friends. The idea that Gwen is a successful business owner in a male-dominated industry would never cross your mind. And there is certainly nothing about her that, at first glance, would lead you to surmise that this woman has seen it all. But from a ship repair yard to a life coach's office to a politician's desk, Gwen's certainly seen more than most.

Life for Gwen began near New Orleans, Louisiana. In her early childhood years of innocence, she played in the fields and the bayous of South Louisiana, living with her mother and brother and surrounded by her cousins on her grandparents' farm. But at the start of World War II, her grandfather was called to serve his country. For him, this duty involved going to work in the shipyards to build ships for the war effort. His absence meant the women would have to leave the farm; there was no way they could manage it without a man's help. So the women packed up and left in the only available vehicle for moving a family: a hearse. Their destination was the city of New Orleans and a rooming house. Shortly after their move, Gwen's mother took a job as a bus driver, while the other women in Gwen's extended family, especially her beloved grandmother and aunt, took care of a total of eight kids in all.

Although money was scarce, happiness and unconditional love were not. The family was united, and Gwen's grandmother, the matriarch, made it her primary objective to value family and faith regardless of circumstances. Gwen's life was filled with school, playing, and her favorite sport—fishing with her brother and cousins. Fishing revealed the first sign of Gwen's competitive spirit. She became a master craftswoman in the art of creating poles and hooks before she was even eight years old. She selected the best pieces of bamboo for her poles with just the right flexibility and strength, and then chose the right safety pins and bent them artfully, the perfect lure for any fish. She also had an eye for worms. She'd dig until she found one with enough wiggle and plumpness to lure her catch, which was then served for dinner. She became the envy of her brother and cousins for her fishing abilities. Gwen, along with everyone else, big and small, contributed to the family's survival, through both play and work. Although Gwen's mother was working and attending nursing school and hence absent in Gwen's life much of the time, her young life was still stable. That is, until her thirteenth year.

At thirteen, Gwen's life took a dramatic turn for the worse. The war had ended, and her mother decided to leave New Orleans for Seattle. She had met and married a man, and they had made Seattle their home. Shortly afterwards, the call came requesting that Gwen and her brother be put on a bus to Seattle for a short vacation with their mother. The truth, however, was a different story: the trip was a permanent one. Gwen and her brother learned after their arrival that they were being uprooted from the safety, security, and happiness of their blended family. Gwen's grandmother and aunt, the two people she had loved dearly and had learned life's lessons and values from, would no longer be central figures in her life. She would be living with her mother—a woman she barely knew—and her new stepfather, a total stranger. Her mother's subterfuge was Gwen's first encounter with deceit and betrayal. Resentment and a deep sense of loss followed her throughout high school.

With her mother working for Boeing and her stepfather employed in a steel mill, the life Gwen had known on the farm in Louisiana had disappeared. What remained in her heart and spirit were the love and the values taught to her by her grandmother and aunt. As Gwen struggled to deal with her emotions, all that she'd been taught still prevented her from doing anything in her teenage years that would hurt her or her family.

By ninth grade, Gwen had settled into her new life and found a boyfriend. Her high school sweetheart in time became her husband and the father to their three children. Having been raised watching both her grandfather and her stepfather work manual labor jobs, Gwen and her husband easily took over the family business: the ship repair company. It wasn't large, but it quickly became a highly respected company not only in the commercial shipping industry of Seattle but also with the U.S. Navy and the U.S. Coast Guard.

As co-owner of a small family business in a male-dominated industry, Gwen proved to be a worthy competitor, whether she was structuring contracts, managing a small but highly efficient office staff, or peering up at welders working on boat hulls and ensuring that their caliber of work matched the company's standards. Quality and efficiency mattered for a small business, and it was Gwen's job to make sure the work was done to the highest standard for the least cost. Many days, however, Gwen's title of "owner" meant nothing. If there was work to do and nobody available to do it, Gwen would jump in. Those many days spent fishing in the Louisiana bayous and competing with the boys for bringing home the most fish set the stage for her future. The skills she had learned then served her far beyond the fishing hole.

Unfortunately, although Gwen and her husband could fix the cracks in ships, they couldn't fix the cracks in their marriage. After thirty-four years of marriage and three children, the fractures in the foundation of their marriage began to widen. In 1992, Gwen and her husband divorced. It was by all accounts a highly civilized divorce, without harsh words and ugly conflicts. They had three daughters along with seven grandchildren, and neither Gwen nor her ex was willing to subject their family to internal warfare. They committed to remaining good, close friends.

Unlike most husband–and–wife businesses, Gwen took over their ship repair business after the divorce, rather than her husband. Surrounded by hardworking, salt-of-the-earth men, Gwen was undaunted. She had managed the business since 1980 and had earned the respect and admiration of her employees and customers. She knew the business and knew how to get the work done right to keep it coming through the door. In 1994, Gwen purchased her former husband's stock and became sole proprietor of a strong and financially stable business. With a good team in place to manage the business's workload, Gwen set off on a new mission.

In the early 1980s, the navy began negotiating—unsuccessfully— with the Port of Seattle to secure Pier 90 and Pier 91 as a home port for an aircraft carrier battle group, which would provide a great opportunity to boost the regional ship repair industry. Washington's Senior Senator Henry Jackson stepped in and offered to help bring the home port to Everett. The navy supported this idea, but the local and regional authorities were not fully on board.

The maritime industry was stunned to observe that community leaders would not cooperate in this important opportunity in a time when there was so little ship repair business available. But Gwen had an idea: the industry could form an organization with the express purpose of revitalizing the maritime industry and getting the home port to Everett. It would be a lot of work and politicking, but she had the passion and the brains to make it happen. She knew from the start that it would have to be a collaborative effort by all the industry stakeholders. Due to her perseverance and cooperative organizing, Maritime Alliance of the Pacific Northwest was born.

The first roadblock to success was Washington's state legislature. Although its male domination has been slowly declining over the past ten years, it was, and still on many levels continues to be, a pseudo- fraternity. Imagine its initial response to a white, Republican female knocking on its door and asking for support of a massive undertaking. But Gwen learned early on in life that rejection, either by fish refusing her bait or by elected officials refusing to negotiate, wasn't the end of the deal. It simply meant—in both cases—that she'd have to get a bigger, juicier worm to entice them to bite the hook. She decided to change direction and make the deal more appealing.

Gwen took her cause to Washington, D.C. There she met with the admirals in charge as well as elected officials and others willing to lend an ear to her pitch and commit their support. This time, her relentless leadership paid off. By 1999, the Port of Everett was under construction. She had become a committed leader through those fourteen years, which had motivated others to jump in and make the campaign a success.

As with most everything in life, there were mixed motives behind Gwen's efforts. The new port would open up fresh business opportunities. Contracts with the government for repairs would provide substantial long-term security for her company. It was never a question that Gwen's small business would end up with a big piece of the repair pie. Gwen's company was the successful bidder on the first multi-year/multi-craft aircraft carrier contract in the Pacific Northwest. It was what everyone had worked so hard for and would be shared by many of the Maritime Alliance members. The investment necessary to provide the amount of manpower, equipment, and management to accomplish this contract was enormous. But the point of multi-year contracts is to give both the contractor and the navy extended time to develop a strong infrastructure to provide ongoing quality support for the fleet.

The navy liked the developed process so much that they cancelled the last year of the contract, instead asking the industry to form a team to expand and enhance the progress that had already been made. Gwen was invited to become part of this "Home Team," the winning group for a five-year, $100-million contract. Gwen's repair shop was slated for 10 percent of the work. This project, however, was not intended for garnering monies, but instead was for catching up with the scant profits made during the first phase of the contract.

In short, things were going to be tight financially. Gwen was about to find out how tight.

As part of the process to satisfy the navy contract, Gwen hired a CPA to help officially oversee her company's finances. After a short time, this new-hire stomped off with no notice. Knowing the importance of keeping on top of difficult cash management, Gwen spent a weekend trying to resume control of that task. That weekend threw Gwen into a devastating tailspin. She had known that they were in financial need of some substantial long-term contracts, but her trusted, longtime financial officer had convinced her that although it would be a stretch, they would not go under. But that was not what Gwen found to be reality. She discovered a stack of unpaid bills, most many months overdue. But worse than those were the notification letters from the Internal Revenue Service (IRS) that her taxes were delinquent. The adviser she had trusted to be truthful had in fact deceived her in a most vicious way. The amount she owed was staggering.

At first, Gwen kept telling herself that what she was seeing on the books was just a bad dream. It couldn't be reality. With all her senses on overload, all she could do was to remind herself to breathe until she could regain her wits. The same dizzying questions kept playing over and over in her mind like a merry-go-round. Nothing had prepared her for this. Shifting from disbelief to anger, and then back again to denial and incredulity, Gwen knew she could trust God to get her through it until all her options were exhausted. She didn't know what to do except to pray for acceptance, strength, and the confidence to see it through. The most critical and immediate question facing Gwen was what to tell her dedicated, trusting employees.

First and foremost, Gwen was determined to do the honorable thing. She explained the dire news to her employees and suggested they find work before the paychecks stopped. She was also honest with her creditors telling them that it looked like her business was going under and she wanted to do everything in her power to miraculously prevent that.

Next she needed to make contact with the IRS. Since her first move had obviously been to terminate her financial officer, she hired a firm to help her grasp the magnitude of her financial damage and help her navigate through the rough waters into calmer seas. While the firm was an asset in many ways, Gwen resisted its instructions not to talk to the IRS. It tried to convince her it was better for experienced negotiators to do the talking than someone inexperienced like Gwen. She might make matters worse, it warned. The firm reminded her she had enough on her plate without adding more to it. Ignoring its pleas to stay in the background, Gwen followed her gut instinct and contacted the IRS.

Being upfront with the IRS was the smartest thing Gwen could have done. She was open with them about the situation itself, how she had discovered it, and her commitment to do the right thing. The IRS worked with her, kept an open line of communication, and in the end settled the judgment. Although it took three years to accomplish the feat, there is no IRS horror story to be told.

The financial devastation to her business, however, was overwhelming and beyond salvage. Gwen was forced to file for Chapter 7 Bankruptcy. Whatever the business had of value was sold. By 2001, her company was dissolved, and Gwen was physically, mentally, and emotionally exhausted. But she was solid in her faith. God had given her the strength, confidence, and wisdom to steer her way through a horrific and unanticipated event—and survive it.

With the ship repair business gone, all that Gwen had ever known as work had vanished. Scared and alone, she again prayed to God for guidance and direction. She had no money and no assets other than her family, friends, and the will to go on. What does a woman do after a successful business collapses on her watch? How does she start over?

Again, God answered her prayers. Drained and needing something positive and fulfilling to do, Gwen received a life coach appointment for Christmas from one of her daughters. It was such a positive experience for Gwen that her daughter suggested she look into becoming a life coach herself. After all, she'd been up against more challenges than most and had come through them successfully. Why wouldn't she be the ideal candidate to help others do likewise? So Gwen went off to life coach school. As she discovered from the first class, it was a perfect fit and triggered her passion for working with youth. Instead of repairing ships, she was now, for many of her clients, repairing lives.

Today, Gwen's love of and experience in politics has provided a new career path. Gwen presently serves in a congressman's district office, experiencing the political process from the inside out. And she continues to help people channel through difficult circumstances, teaching the lessons she's learned along the way.

❦   ❦   ❦

Author's Observations:

When Gwen's business that she had dedicated her life to building collapsed in front of her eyes, she recognized that harboring the natural feelings of anger and resentment would only hurt her and would serve no real purpose. She dug herself out of her devastation through her faith in God and her belief that the loss of her business was meant to be, for a reason and purpose not yet understood. She began to open her heart and mind to new opportunities. Starting a new life took courage she didn't even know she had within her until she faced her adversities head on. She discovered that whatever we do in our lives—including both our successes and our failures—serves as preparation for what's yet to come. Gwen took what she'd learned from the past and used it to build her future.

CHAPTER FOUR

JOY

MEET JOY TRAPP[1]. At first glance, Joy wouldn't seem to qualify for this book, since she has earned prominence within the Department of Health and Human Services. However, she gained this reputation not just as an extraordinary employee, but as a client—one with a long history of serious, repetitive problems.

Joy was born in Tacoma, Washington, into a life that would be filled with chaos and confusion. Her mother left her father and remarried shortly before Joy's birth. Although Joy maintained contact with her natural father, theirs was not a relationship of unconditional love. In fact, from the beginning she never made the mark with either of her parents or her stepfather. She was one of those kids labeled "trouble." Her younger brother and only sibling, on the other hand, was the antithesis. He was a good kid and was rewarded correspondingly, while Joy seemed to be punished simply for being alive. Nothing she did—or didn't do—was "right," and her actions and accomplishments went unnoticed at home and in school. Not only was she a problem child, looking for opportunities to create turmoil and conflict, she was black. Joy was convinced that her Caucasian stepfather held being black, looking black, against her.

---
[1]All names other than Joy's have been changed to protect the individuals' identities.

Because her light-skinned mother could pass for white, it was all the more obvious that Joy was not his biological child. Along with Joy's troubled relationship with her stepfather, she had great contempt for her alcoholic mother. Home was in a constant state of unrelenting hatred and resentment, and it was not a place she intended to be any longer than was absolutely necessary. At a young age, she obsessively began planning her escape.

As Joy recalls it, nobody ever offered a positive or encouraging word to her, at home or in school, until she met her fifth-grade physical education teacher. Observing Joy's compulsion to misbehave and act tough, while also noticing that she was lean, strong, and fast, she suggested that she put some of that energy into doing something positive. "Why don't you give track a try?" she asked. "You could excel, make something of yourself, if you'd give it a shot." No one had ever suggested that she could be talented at anything, but hearing she could be a star if she put forth the effort was all the motivation she needed. She began to imagine doing something well, doing something right. She wanted to feel what it would be like to succeed at something and hear her parents' praise. Finally she had hope for finding love and acceptance.

True to her word, her teacher began working with her, grooming her to be a star athlete. In no time, Joy was running and competing—and winning. She quickly learned to embrace the thrill of victory on the track, but the defeat she continued to experience at home was insurmountable. Neither her mother nor her stepfather acknowledged her newfound success, instead continuing to focus on what was wrong with her and reminding her of her failures. As she moved on to the sixth grade, track meets became part of the past. In a new environment, with no encouragement from home and no cheerleading teacher in her corner, her sense of worthlessness returned. Joy picked up where she left off and was back on the road to self-destruction. The words of her parents, including those of her biological father, echoed in her mind: "You'll never amount to anything." This hopeless mantra played over and over in her head until she thought, why try? What's the use? No one else cares, why should I?

The ongoing friction between Joy and her family continued to become more and more unmanageable. At fourteen, Joy became pregnant, which culminated in an abortion at her mother's insistence. She was now a statistic, and although she didn't grow up in poverty, she nonetheless felt deprived of love and support—a far worse affliction than lack of money. When she turned sixteen, she became pregnant again. Unsurprisingly, this news was not received well; both her family and her school wanted her out. It was 1978—there were no special arrangements for pregnant students. Since she couldn't manage both a baby and school anyway, Joy became another statistic: an eleventh-grade dropout and an unwed teenage mother.

Joy promptly moved in with Ed, the baby's nineteen-year-old father. Predictably, it didn't last long; a child raising a child was a bad mix. By the time Natalie was born, Joy found she was longing for some emotional guidance and direction from her own mother. She left Ed and headed for home with her two-month-old baby in tow, hoping things would be different. But as she discovered, that hope was futile. Nothing had changed. She was again reminded of her flaws and her failures constantly. Sick and tired of her stepfather's expectations of servitude and afraid of her own heightened resentment and hatred toward her parents, Joy moved out. She immediately contacted social services for a foster home for Natalie and began working part-time jobs and living anywhere with anyone who'd take her in. This arrangement lasted about a year. Within the first year of Natalie's life, she had been in and out of three different foster homes. Natalie's fragile future hung in the balance, and Joy was smart enough to know this life wasn't good for her baby. Desperate to save her child from being bounced around, Joy and her mother agreed to try it again. Living with her mother was bad, but she'd try to bite the bullet and put up with the grief for the sake of her daughter.

Reality quickly set in. Joy didn't belong there, but this time there was a change. Joy's mother discovered that being a mother to her grandchild was easier than being one to her own daughter. They agreed to do what was in the best interest of the baby: Natalie would stay with her grandmother, and Joy would leave and head to Seattle to find work. This time she settled down and landed a full-time job with a law firm, quickly discovering that she was not adverse to work. It was a milestone for Joy, and once she'd mastered her assigned duties, she was off in search of better jobs and higher pay.

By 1981, Natalie was still with her grandmother and doing well. Joy, on the other hand, had met the father of what would become her second child, another daughter, Josephine, born in 1982. Six months after the baby was born, they married. Unfortunately for everyone, though, what seemed at first to be a good marriage swiftly turned into a nightmare. Life with her new husband eventually became centered around one word—terror. Joy discovered too late that she had married a violent man. With no provocation, he'd use her as his punching bag, which was a first for her. As bad as life had been up to that point, it had never been a physically abusive or violent one. Verbal berating she was used to, but this was a whole new abuse. She had to get out before he killed her—literally. Because he kept her in his sights at all times, devising a plan of escape was a monumental challenge. But she found a rare opportunity one day, after he had gone out to run some errands. She bolted with Josephine in tow and never looked back.

Once again, her world was crashing in around her. Terrified and hopeless, Joy wound up at Seattle Mental Health. It was there that she learned about the roots and signs of domestic violence. Like many women, she tried to learn what to look out for and how to detect abusers. Confident in her knowledge, she met and married Daniel. He appeared to be a good man, not prone to violence—at least that's what she thought before she married him and had two more children. Now, at twenty-five, Joy was the mother of four children in yet another bad marriage that had all the elements of a disaster in the making. There were drugs involved now, and even after her counseling at Seattle Mental Health, she was faced with more domestic violence, including her first emergency room visit. Faced again with the daunting task of leaving a marriage, this one having lasted ten years, she made her getaway and headed back to

Tacoma. This time her home was not at her mother's, but instead at a shelter for victims of domestic violence.

It was during this time that Joy realized she had an obsession with hate and resentment. Ever so slowly, this obsession turned to thoughts of acting upon these two very destructive emotions. She'd spend endless hours thinking of how wronged she had been: her failed marriages, four children she couldn't care for, and parents who had emotionally and physically rejected her. Add to that a mother she'd not seen sober in years, her seemingly perfect brother, and her former violent, substance-abusing husbands. Feeling sorry for herself and blaming others for her misery, her thoughts turned to killing her mother and her stepfather (who has since passed away). If she could get rid of them, she thought, just maybe the pain would ease. With any luck, it just might go away completely.

But two things stood in the way of taking this drastic action and living with the despair that would inevitably follow: her four children and the promise of prison time. She desperately wanted to bring all her children back under one roof and provide for them, and prison time would be the end of that dream. Accompanying that hope was her knowledge that somewhere, somehow, there was a God. Somewhere deep in her soul, covered by layers upon layers of hatred, she knew God existed. How He existed for her, Joy did not know. After all, if her own parents found her unlovable, and husbands thought she was disposable and deserving of attack, how could God love her? Still, it was her shallow belief—but a belief nonetheless—that vengeful murder was certainly not going to be met with God's approval. She wasn't the worst of the worst, so why try to be? Joy finally pushed her murderous thoughts out of her mind, but she continued to wonder just how unworthy of love she really was. Her successful track meets and especially her four children were great accomplishments. Why couldn't her family and her past lovers spare her some kind words? Even just one word would do, after twenty-five years of virtually none.

In 1985, at thirty-three years of age and looking again for acceptance and love in the wrong places, Joy tried again, packing up her daughters (including Natalie, pregnant at seventeen) and following her new husband to Dallas (her son, fathered by Daniel, stayed behind to live with him in Seattle). This time her marriage lasted for two years. But anger still filled her spirit and her soul. Anger and marriage are seldom compatible, which she quickly proved. With more physical abuse in the mix—including a torturous four-hour ordeal of him threatening to slit her throat—Joy divorced again. She was mastering relationship failure.

Having left her latest ex-husband behind, she landed back in Seattle with her daughters. To help resolve the problems of no money, no job, and no place to live, Joy decided to visit a church. What better place to find solutions to these material problems? But Joy found more than money…she found an awakened, active belief in God. She absorbed the belief that God loved her and that she was worthy of His love, regardless of her sins and many failures. It was the first hope she'd had since her days of running track. She wanted, from the depths of her soul, to believe that the Lord saw her through different eyes than all the others in her life. If God loved her, and if she really believed it, then maybe the cycle of despair and bad decisions, including jumping from one relationship to another looking for genuine love, would end. Faith was her only chance; nothing else had worked. Had the Lord led her here to this place at this time in her life? Had He been waiting for her to get tired of doing it her way? Joy believed so. A recognition of deep, unbridled faith in the Lord and all that He wanted her to be would become the defining moment in her life and in the lives of her children. Things would change, but not before she accepted God in every fiber of her body and soul. That would take time…and a few more unwise choices.

During this time, Joy received some good news: she was offered a job at Wal-Mart and finally found meaningful employment. It was the first time she had a position in which she could prove herself, get noticed by the management, and be rewarded with more money and promotions. This job marked the beginning of her newfound confidence and self-esteem. Could it be that this was the Lord's way of showing her He did love her? With His help, she was beginning to believe she could remake herself to be the person He had intended her to be. She simply had to do her part and not wallow in pity, hoping for change.

Yet all was not perfect. Joy met and married another man, this time a Native American who was ten years her elder. He seemed like the perfect fit, but after settling down with him, she soon discovered that the man she married was not the same man she had dated. She had looked but had failed to see the signs that another disaster was unfolding. Within months of their union, he told Joy that with the marriage license in hand, he had "bought" her. "I own you. You belong to me." He treated her as if she were a piece of property, no different than the car he owned. He dictated her every movement. She couldn't believe she'd fallen into an abusive situation again. This time, however, was different. She was no longer the helpless victim she had been in the past.

By this point in her life, Joy had gained some confidence in her work skills and had begun to embrace the idea of doing a good job and being rewarded accordingly. In a stroke of good fortune, her next reward came from none other than the school district. They offered her a job she couldn't refuse, with more money and higher status. Before leaving for Dallas, Joy had earned her G.E.D. and now it was paying off. She left Wal-Mart and went back to the very place she'd been thrown out of almost twenty years earlier, when pregnant with her first child. She was making huge progress in her work life. Her personal life, however, still had to catch up.

Again, Joy headed to divorce court, this time after ten years of absolute control by a man who didn't love her. Regrettably, though, he controlled their finances. Their home was declared his and his alone by the courts. She faced a choice between staying and living with the abuse or leaving with nothing but the clothes on her back and her youngest daughter, now fifteen. Homelessness was not the life she wanted for her daughter. But after experiencing the thrill of accomplishment and success at work and gaining a sense of herself and her own value, she knew she could not stay married to a man who constantly demeaned and degraded her. Getting out became her total focus. After making some calls, Joy and her daughter temporarily moved in with a friend willing to open her home to them. Although she was told that it would not be a permanent solution, Joy had assumed they could stay at least until she could earn enough money to rent an apartment. She was therefore dismayed to learn that her friend had had enough of houseguests after only two weeks. Joy realized that after spending ten years with gainful employment and a relatively stable home, she and her daughter were homeless. It was devastating to Joy to comprehend the magnitude of the impact this had on her soul. Again, she questioned the Lord's love for her and His will in her life. "How could this be?" She asked herself this question over and over again, drenched in tears, scared, desperate, and beyond hopeless.

Sitting on a curb with her daughter, ashamed to look her in the eyes, Joy became, for the first time in her life, truly enraged. Her anger wasn't targeted toward her parents, her ex-husbands, or her brother being so perfect. Instead, it was directed at herself. But her faith in the Lord translated that anger into a force for change. "I'm worth more than this," she heard herself say. "I don't deserve to live like this, and neither does my daughter. I can make something of myself, and I will." In short, Joy was fed up with being fed up. It was no longer about other people and what they did or didn't do. It was about stopping the cycle of despair and destruction. It was about saving herself and her daughter.

After this conversation with herself, she told a girlfriend about the declaration she'd made about who she was and what she deserved. She had already demonstrated she was willing to work and earn her way through life. She wasn't looking for handouts, but rather just a helping hand. Hearing this, her friend suggested she speak with someone at Washington Women in Need (WWIN), a nonprofit organization founded by Julia Pritt to help women in need who want to rebuild their lives. Its mission is to provide women with medical, dental, educational, or counseling resources in order to get them back on their feet. Joy's faith gave her strength, but she still had to learn to love herself on her own. So instead of lashing out at everyone in her life as she had done in the past, Joy contacted WWIN, reaching out for a hand to help her pull herself up. WWIN discovered what Joy's fifth-grade teacher had observed: here was a woman for whom life had dealt a bad hand, and who had no idea how to transform it into a good one. Colloquially, she didn't know how to turn lemons into lemonade. What she had done, over and over, was to take a bad hand and deal herself an even worse hand. This pattern had to change.

WWIN provided a grant for one year of mental health counseling, something Joy desperately needed. In addition, it agreed to fund her college education that she so passionately wanted. For a woman whose own parents said she would never amount to anything, the seemingly unattainable chance to get a higher education suddenly became one of the most important gifts Joy would ever receive. It was, as Joy in her jubilation of gratitude acknowledges, a gift from the Lord. She had done nothing to deserve this generosity other than show up and ask for help to not repeat old behaviors. She'd simply asked for a chance to build a life she'd be proud of.

All WWIN could do for Joy was provide her with the opportunity for a better life; it was up to Joy to use its benevolence to make a better life for herself. Its gifts of counseling and tuition monies for college meant nothing unless Joy made a commitment to not abuse or misuse its generosity and the faith it had in her. And she didn't let them down. She stuck with counseling until she understood why she was attracted to dysfunctional men, why she was so angry, and how she could use her anger more constructively—to her benefit rather than to her detriment. Counseling would also aid her as she learned to manage day-to-day life, facing its omnipresent challenges and obstacles. Her counselor became her guide, her coach, and her mentor. As the months passed, Joy found herself making better decisions and solving problems more skillfully. She abandoned her old tendencies toward denial and blame. She was no longer a victim, but instead an opportunist. She embraced her education and began to flourish in college. Each small milestone was a huge leap for a woman who'd spent forty years of her life convinced she was born to fail. She was succeeding on all fronts, one step at a time. The added blessing for her was the example she was setting for her four children. She could show them that their lives might be anything but normal and that mistakes will always be made, but that it's never too late to change. The future holds new days filled with opportunity if one is committed to stopping the cycle of destruction and self-pity.

Joy was finally free—free from living with despair and failure, free from the bitter ties of anger and resentment, and free from wallowing in her own misfortune. She had found the conviction that the Lord loved her even when she couldn't love herself. He had always been there for her, even when her sense of unworthiness prevented her from asking for His help. When she was ready, He led her to a place where the doors to a better life opened wide. He helped her find the courage to start anew.

Today, Joy has remarried. This time, she has helped to create a marriage rooted in love and a mutual faith in the Lord. She has also gone on to earn her B.A. degree from Evergreen State College. Joy has committed her life to helping other women in need through her position as a counselor for a non-profit organization. She works with women who have lived lives full of hopelessness and despair. Who better to serve this needy segment of our population but someone who has lived it, felt it, and—finally—survived it?

Joy is living proof to her clients that it doesn't matter where you come from; what matters is where you're going. Her courage to believe it wasn't too late to start over and leave a worthy legacy for her children and grandchildren gave her the push she needed to make a real life for herself. "Anything is attainable if your heart says I can do it and I must do it," Joy explains with conviction. Most importantly, Joy has learned, with regard to both others as well as herself, how to forgive.

Author's Observations:

Joy's courage to stop blaming others for her own reckless choices and to accept and forgive the past enabled her to become the extraordinary woman she is today. Letting go of prior failures and reaching out for help, all the while learning to believe in herself, contributed to her knowledge that she could make something of herself. Her burgeoning faith convinced her that God intended her to be a contributor to society, not a burden. Today, with her mother and her kids as her biggest supporters, she has left a legacy for her children to inherit. Joy is living proof that it's never too late to pick yourself up, take a good, hard look at your life, and make a change.

CHAPTER FIVE

PAT

MEET PAT RUTLEDGE. She's a petite blonde, 5'3" tall, with big blue eyes and a smile that can warm an unheated room in the dead of winter. Seldom will you find her without her four-legged companion, Bogey, a Silky Terrier as energetic and outgoing as Pat. She and her husband of thirty-one years, Richard, are lifelong residents of the greater Seattle Eastside in Washington. Collectively, they have six children: two from Pat's first and short-lived marriage and four from Richard's. Blending two families together early in their adult lives proved to be the first of their marital challenges as well as the beginning of what would become their fortified, unbreakable union. Adversity and challenges are no strangers to this couple. But talk with Pat for a few minutes, and you'll discover that within her vivacious personality is a woman with unwavering optimism and faith that all will work out if you don't give up when the going gets tough. She is the eternal optimist, the rock, the one whose faith keeps their lives together no matter how challenging circumstances are from day to day. These were fortunate characteristics to have, since this deep faith and optimism would be put to the ultimate test fifteen years into their marriage.

Following her graduation from high school, Pat married and had two children in quick succession. But after ten disappointing and dysfunctional years of marriage, Pat filed for divorce, which left her as the primary provider for her children. Well-paying jobs for a woman with only a high school diploma and two children were scarce, leaving Pat with few options other than waitressing. Undaunted, Pat had learned early on that life being fair was far from a guarantee. Whining about circumstances was not in her character; she'd do what she could with the cards she was dealt. This strong and admirable character trait would serve her well years down the road. She had grit and believed she was owed nothing unless she earned it—a defining characteristic in her ability to turn ordinary jobs into extraordinary opportunities. Pat became a waitress in the only five-star restaurant in the Seattle area at the time. Her personality and work ethic gave her the reputation of being one of the best servers and, in turn, earned her bountiful tips. Her salary exceeded that of many of her well-educated customers, much to her delight. In addition to a good income, Pat had the perfect work schedule for a single mother needing to be home with her children. Her loyal customers and their generous tips sustained Pat and her children through her time as a single parent.

After two years of singlehood, Pat was introduced to Richard. After a year's courtship, they married and happily joined their two families: Pat with a boy and a girl, and Richard with three girls and a boy. They also began to explore their true passions in life, especially Richard's. During high school, Richard had become an avid and passionate golfer. While other kids were doing homework or goofing off in study hall, Richard could be found doodling golf course designs. His dream was to design, build, and own a golf course. But in order to earn a living after graduating, he gravitated into the sign-making business. He became a master sign designer and craftsman, and when he and Pat met, the first major decision he made was to start his own sign business. Pat fully supported his decision and became his bookkeeper.

By 1975, Pat's plate was overflowing with responsibilities. Being a full-time wife and mother to two children and a part-time stepmother to four wasn't enough work for her, so she decided to give hairstyling a try. She enrolled with her teenage daughter in cosmetology school. Together, they successfully completed the coursework and received their respective certifications. Hairstyling would offer her flexible hours just as being a waitress had, and it also would allow her to dedicate time each week for her and her husband to spend together, something not enough couples do. This time was spent on their now joint passion, introduced to Pat by Richard at the onset of their courtship: golf. Pat became hooked on the game immediately. Richard's dream of owning a course soon became a mutual goal.

As the years passed, with their kids grown and gone with their own children, more free time meant more time for golf. And the more they played, the more intense their passion became for the game. With her husband's job success, their secured investments, "big boy" toys in the garage and parked around the house, and a vacation home on the water, Pat retired from hairstyling and dedicated her free time to perfecting her golf game. But all that changed one day in May of 1988. Richard had just returned from Scotland where he and three buddies, all golf course owners, had spent a week playing at some of the world's oldest and most renowned golf courses. His dream of forty years—designing, building, and owning a golf course—took root and came alive during the trip. His three friends encouraged him to go for it during the many hours they spent talking about the business of golf. One promised to be his mentor if he'd do it. "Do it now, Richard!" was their common refrain. Fifty years of age had come and gone, and retirement wasn't far off. Convinced his friends were right that it was now or never, Richard spent the nine-hour flight home to Seattle designing his dream course—a real one this time. He also started his list of things to do, prioritizing each item. He couldn't wait to tell Pat the news.

Pat embraced his news enthusiastically. But unbeknownst to either of them, their predictable, secure life was about to end. The challenges that lay ahead would test them like they'd never been tested before. What they thought would be a time of pure joy while building the golf course of their dreams would instead turn into a nightmare, the likes of which they never could have anticipated.

With their business plan in place, they needed to start making decisions. Richard closed his sign business so he could devote all his time and energy to the project. There was a lot of work to do: permits and environmental issues to be resolved, dirt to move, trees to plant, water and drainpipes to be laid, greens to build, grass to plant and nurture, and parking lots and a clubhouse to build. The list was endless, but two years seemed like a reasonable estimate from start to finish. Pat would keep the books, manage the project expenses, outfit the clubhouse, stock the snack bar, and interview vendors and potential employees. The amount of work was monumental, but they didn't care. It was about making their dream come alive, almost like bringing a child into the world. The anticipation of opening day was like preparing for a birth. They envisioned wall-to-wall cars in the parking lot, people laughing, golfers making excuses for their bad scores, talk of rematches…people, young and old, having fun. The talk of what was to come filled their home with abounding excitement and enthusiasm.

One of the major issues facing them was where to build their golf course. They needed to find a place that was accessible, picturesque, and affordable. On the day Richard discovered such a place, he couldn't contain his excitement. The land was just over one hundred acres, located in Fall City, Washington. It was only a half hour east of Seattle, easily reachable for golfers, and only a few miles away from their own home. A river running alongside it and a view of snowcapped mountains for golfers to enjoy perfected their dream beyond their imagination. It also had access to plenty of water, which would not only add to the serenity but would also make it easy to keep the fairways green. Everything was falling into place. The next step was striking a deal with its owners.

To make the golf course design work, they needed to buy two adjoining parcels of land. Two owners were sharing a common border, with a river flowing across both boundaries. It was classified as an agricultural zone, and both were inhabited by grazing cows. Pat and Richard needed to convince the owners to sell their property. What was expected to be a challenge quickly turned into an opportunity. Both landowners agreed to lease the land to Pat and Richard for fifty years, eliminating the need to borrow money to buy the land. One of the landowners made an offer that Richard and Pat couldn't refuse. Because of his confidence in the golf course's success and his prior business experience, he put cash into the venture on top of leasing his land, increasing his investment and his shares. Tom and Eleanor, Richard's brother and sister-in-law, wanted in on the new endeavor too. Tom had retired from his job as an air traffic controller and had money to invest. The partnership grew from two to four within a month.

Pat and Richard sold off their assets, vacation home, toys, and all their investments; in short, they sold everything they had except their primary residence in order to finance the golf course. They were committed and controlling partners. So far everything was falling into place. With continued good fortune, in less than two years they and the golfing public would be playing on their new course. Richard worked and reworked his design until he got it just right. He'd drawn the smallest details imaginable, even scrubs and trees, tee boxes, and benches. Life was too good to be true. This forty-year dream of Richard's was now within arm's length. What, they wondered, had they done to deserve a piece of heaven on earth?

Unfortunately, life rarely goes as planned. Richard and Pat had anticipated some obstacles along the way, but they certainly never could have imagined what would come their way next.

With the assets sold, land leases signed, and money in the bank, the permit application process began in earnest in 1989. By the time the mounds of paperwork were submitted and the permit and legal fees were paid, they were closing in on one year—more time than they had anticipated. Pat and Richard had believed they'd be well on their way to a grand opening by now, not stuck waiting to get the permit process initiated. By the end of year one, no progress had been made, and well into year two the situation remained static. No permits were issued, just requests for more documentation, more studies, and more money. The delay began to drain them financially and emotionally. They needed more money, and they needed it fast. Their cash reserves had taken a big hit, and the money dedicated for construction began to dwindle. They'd already sold all their assets. They realized the only thing they had left to sell was their house.

They'd have to drain the equity out of it in order to stay afloat and bring in some income.

Pat resumed hairstyling for grocery money, while Richard picked up some sign business work for extra income. The house was gone; they were living in a 60' x 40' cold and barren trailer, a far cry from their former 4,000-square-foot spacious and inviting home. The only thing that they could count on now was mounting debt. They poured every dollar they made into keeping themselves and the costly permit process alive.

By the end of the second year, nothing had changed. No permits issued, no permits denied—just more money and time demanded by the county. The only thing that did change was the number of partners. Early into year two, the landowner opted out, unwilling to continue to pour money down what appeared to be a bottomless sinkhole. To Richard and Pat's horror, a third grueling year began and ended with no progress by the county.

With one partner gone and Tom on the precipice of bailing out as well, they soldiered on. They were too far into it to pull out now, they decided. Besides, it was their dream they were fighting for. How could it get any worse? They asked themselves this question over and over as each day passed unchanged. Pat's faith and optimism that the end had to be in sight kept their hope alive. But time was running out. If the situation didn't turn in their favor quickly, their dream would be over, and financial recovery would be virtually impossible.

By now, a different problem was starting to take its toll on Richard and Pat other than just debt. Richard's personality was beginning to change. A typically upbeat guy, he had become worn down emotionally over the last few years. He slowly drifted into what would become a deep depression. He spent hours roaming the property, visualizing what could have or should have been, while fearing the worst. He blamed himself and withdrew from Pat, repeatedly asking himself the same questions. Was he just stupid or too stubborn? How could he have put the woman he loved through this? Why didn't he listen to all those people who warned him about the permit process and the endless studies and delays? Was he so blinded by his dream that he failed to see reality? They were now flat broke. Richard dreaded looking his wife in the eyes. Pat, in turn, held on by her thread of faith and believed they would prevail. It tormented her to look into her husband's eyes only to see the life and vitality draining out of a once happy and carefree man. She was starting to become afraid he'd do something extreme, perhaps even take his own life.

Pat's only respite from the despair and the fear as year three turned into year four was her courage to reach deep within her soul and believe, against all odds, that everything would be okay, whatever the outcome. If for no other reason, she kept the faith for Richard. She could go back to cutting hair full time, and Richard could go back to his sign-making career. They'd survive even if all else was lost. As she reminded Richard that they'd survive it together, she was also buoying her own spirits and optimism.

Pat does admit to making a huge mistake during their nightmare: withdrawal. They chose to avoid their friends and not burden them with their problems. They isolated themselves, making their burdens even heavier. They severed their invaluable resources for encouragement, laughter, and love. Cutting off this lifeline of support that their friends wanted to provide for them made an already difficult situation that much more arduous.

Well into another agonizing year, a meeting was scheduled with the county. Pat and Richard had agreed, finally, that this was the last chance for them. Richard said he would attend, but only to tell the decision makers that he was through. He'd also tell them how the last four years had devastated them. He'd explain how they could deal with any decision, good or bad, but not more indecision. After all the meeting attendees were seated, Richard stood up and stated what he had planned. He told them how he and his wife had lost everything, explained that they were deep in debt, and exhaustedly declared that the stagnant project had destroyed them, both financially and personally. He finished, thanked them for listening, and left the room, which was eerily silent as he departed. In Richard's heart as he walked the endless corridor to the elevator, he was certain he had just blown any chance of getting the necessary permits approved. His lawyer, attending with him, confirmed that he had most likely sealed their fate. It was over. He'd have to tell Pat, he thought, but how? Between bouts of tears, he realized they'd have to figure out how to recover from a seemingly impossible situation.

But life held one more big surprise for Richard and Pat. Richard had asked that the county listen that day, and they did. Within three months' time, Richard and Pat were notified that a deal had been struck—the permits were approved, issued, and ready to be picked up. A golf course would be built.

Ecstatic, Pat and Richard, with permits in hand and spirits renewed, notified Tom and Eleanor that construction could begin immediately. Richard and Tom turned the dirt, laid the irrigation and drainage systems, planted trees, built greens, nurtured new grass, put in a clubhouse and paved parking lots. Pat took her list and worked it methodically. Seven days a week, day and night, they worked. Of course, they denied that it was "work" at all. For them, it was a labor of love.

Memorial Day, 1994, was a historic day. Twin Rivers Golf Course opened its doors to the public. A dream and a miracle were born, confirmed by the rainbow that arched its way across the entire course on opening day—a sign that dreams do come true, faith and persistence do matter, and a woman's courage should never be underestimated.

And what's forty years of waiting for a dream to materialize as you cast a glance over your shoulder at the dedicated and happy golfers playing your course?

🌿   🌿   🌿

Author's Observations:

Pat had a fiercely loyal commitment to Richard and their marriage, and she knew that material possessions, while nice to have, did not define them. The vision of their dream realized, along with the backbone of their children's and grandchildren's love, supported Pat and Richard to get them through even their blackest days. Pat's innate strength, abiding courage, and unwavering optimism allowed her to navigate both herself and her husband through each difficult day with faith and hope.

CHAPTER SIX

CONNIE

MEET CONNIE OZMER. Like many of us, she and her husband, Tymm, have spent the last seventeen years building their careers and their family. It's fair to say that their lives have taken an unexpected course since high school. Connie and Tymm were high school sweethearts for all of seven months in Connie's junior year before Tymm, a year ahead of her, graduated. He joined the army after graduation while Connie waited faithfully for his visits when on leave from his duty station in Germany. Most memorable was Tymm's return for her senior prom. Love and devotion to one another took root during those early years of dating and has never weakened. The challenges that lay ahead for them, however, would test their strength and commitment like they never could have imagined.

Connie began life in a state of flux. Her mother divorced Connie's father while pregnant with Connie. Soon thereafter, both her parents remarried, each one getting five more children in the process, giving Connie the uncommon distinction of being a stepsister to ten siblings. Both parents were committed to raising their children in harmony versus hatred, and they were equally active in her life. Fortunately for Connie, she was raised in close proximity to both parents in a semirural farming community called Yakima, a hundred miles east of Seattle across the Cascade Mountains. Yakima—a fertile valley best known for its orchards, fruit, hops for beer, grapes for wine, and assorted vegetables—is considered by many to be an ideal environment in which to raise children. Yakima is also known for its Army Regional Training Center. The semidesert terrain, hills and valleys, and extreme weather conditions make it a perfect location for training soldiers, both those of the U.S. Army and the National Guard.

Because of the military presence and its contribution to the economy of the region, patriotism is a point of pride for most inhabitants of Yakima, including its children. Contrary to those of its hub city, Seattle, Yakima folks are shameless in their support for our nation's armed forces. This is evident by its strong ROTC program, which provided the military impetus for Tymm. Connie was not only exposed to the community's military pride, but she had also grown up amongst a family in which serving one's country had been a long-standing part of its heritage. When Connie began dating Tymm, it was a perfect match right from the beginning. The fact that Tymm was joining the army made their union not only a good fit, but also a point of pride for their families.

When Tymm returned home for Christmas in 1988, after two years in Germany, his relationship with Connie blossomed into more than a typical youthful love. They discovered they had much in common and that together they were a good fit. Spending their lives together made sense to both of them. As soon as his Christmas leave was up, Tymm would be heading to Fort Benning, Georgia, for his final two years of service. But before he left, he asked Connie to marry him. Unhesitatingly, she said yes. But the length of the engagement was unclear. Because Connie was devoted to obtaining her degree at the University of Washington in Seattle, and Tymm was committed to two more years in the army stationed in Georgia, no date was set.

Once the holidays had passed, it was time for Tymm to make the long drive from Washington back to the army base in Georgia, and he wanted Connie to join him. She was back in school but figured she could easily miss a week and a half to make the trip and could catch up quickly upon her return. She agreed to go along for the ride.

Tymm, although having lived in Yakima since the second grade, was originally from Tennessee. Virtually all of his extended family still lived there, and he wanted to stop there first to proudly introduce his bride-to-be.

As he drove the route back to his hometown, Tymm's mind began going into overdrive. Knowing that his family wouldn't be able to make the long trip to Washington for a wedding, Tymm devised a plan. Why not, he pondered during the monotonous hours of watching asphalt go by, have two weddings? It made sense. They could have a wedding now in Tennessee. Tymm's brother wouldn't have to travel to Washington; he'd have the privilege of being Tymm's best man at his home. Later, they could have a second wedding in Washington to celebrate their union, once life had calmed down a bit. With his plan and the details figured out, he shared his notion with Connie en route. Madly in love with him, she agreed it was an outstanding idea. They'd marry now, and Tymm would finish out his two years at Fort Benning and return to Washington. Connie would go back to college and would only have a year left by the time Tymm returned for good. Then they could focus on a second wedding in Yakima.

Connie and Tymm did as planned, marrying in a civil ceremony during their brief stop in Tennessee with Tymm's brother and sister-in-law witnessing the exciting event. Within days, the happy newlyweds arrived in Georgia. Tymm, now a married man, settled in the army barracks, and Connie returned to Seattle to complete her education, keeping their big secret. When the time was right, she'd let her family know that she and Tymm were now husband and wife. But now was not the right time. Her education, not marriage, was her family's priority for her. The news would not be embraced. But, like with most secrets, it was revealed sooner than she had anticipated.

As frequently happens, their seemingly well-thought-out plans and real life collided. Within a week of returning to school, not only was separation from Tymm too painful, but studying and classes became torturous as Connie's thoughts drifted away from school and onto Tymm and their future together. A new plan was devised to remedy their longing for each other. Tymm, they knew, could not just walk away from the army. He was stuck for two more years. Connie, on the other hand, could walk away from school. It wouldn't please her parents, but she knew their love for her would eventually win them over. She called her mother and asked her to pick her and her belongings up from school. She then announced that she was moving to Georgia to be with Tymm. Her mother, shocked and confused, hesitatingly agreed to pick her daughter up, or at least drive to Seattle to reason with her. Her mother and sister made the three-hour trip to Seattle from Yakima. After sharing her words of wisdom and warnings about her decision, her mother quickly discovered that Connie's mind was made up. Most distressing to her mother was that Connie, still assumed to be unmarried, would be living with her boyfriend. That was an unacceptable plan, she lectured. Next on her list was Connie's education. Why, she asked, would Connie throw her education away for a boy? Her mother pleaded that if Connie wouldn't change her mind about her decision, the least she and Tymm could do was get married.

Torn between being honest and maintaining their secret, Connie chose honesty. She told her mother and sister the truth. "We're already married," she confessed. Her mother did what most mothers would do: she got mad—really mad. Mothers imagine, often in great detail, momentous events that will happen in their children's lives from birth to marriage, and beyond. This, however, was not the wedding day she'd imagined for her daughter for the past nineteen years. She'd dreamt of her daughter with her degree behind her, walking down the center aisle of a church with her proud parents embracing the moment. Her vision of what that day would hold was no longer a possibility.

Thankfully, though, mothers are resilient. Anger was short-lived as reality began to sink in. She didn't like what had happened, but she understood it. And besides, what choice did she have but to accept it? During the course of their conversation, rather than harboring anger and resentment, she wisely let her infuriation dissipate. Her love had always been unconditional, and it would be so now. She vowed to not only support and embrace her daughter but to do likewise for her new son-in-law. She'd give them both a good start toward a lasting finish.

The day before Connie flew out of Seattle and headed for the arms of her new husband, her mother arranged for a bridal shower for her daughter. Connie's send-off and the acceptance of her marriage by her mother were better than Connie could have imagined. She truly felt like a new bride venturing off to start a fresh life, surrounded by the love of family and friends.

Although Connie and Tymm had much in common, there was a significant difference between them. Their immediate goals were conflicting. Connie, now living happily with her husband, found herself coming back to her desire for a college education and was determined to finish what she'd started. Connie was also adamant about Tymm completing his education after the army. Tymm, on the other hand, wanted to start a family immediately, believing that his education could follow. Finally, after many discussions on the subject of which goal should come first, Connie's wish for them to secure their educations before adding the joy and added responsibility of children prevailed.

After two years of marriage and four years of service to his country, Tymm, along with his wife, returned to Yakima. They enrolled in the local community college and worked part time to pay their living expenses. They graduated with their associate's degrees and then applied, and were accepted, to Western Washington University. Connie majored in management information systems, while Tymm chose to major in literature. With grants, loans, and Tymm's GI Bill covering most of their academic expenses, they still needed to work part time to make ends meet. By the time they received their degrees, Tymm had decided to stay on for another two years. He was accepted into graduate school to earn his Master of Education (M.Ed.), and Connie went to work full time for AT&T Wireless as a Web developer. While it sounds simple enough—one spouse in college and the other working—it wasn't. Connie faced a commute of one hundred miles, one way, to work. They settled on making their home at half the distance between school and work so the drive would be equal for both of them. It was a simple and manageable solution for the two years while Tymm completed his education. Their willingness and ability to make life and its challenges work as best they can had been proven repeatedly by now. And after a few weeks of adjusting to the long commute, they settled into a routine. But their routine would not last for long.

During Tymm's last year of graduate school, Connie discovered she was pregnant. Tymm's dream of having children came to fruition with the birth of their daughter, Emily. Between Tymm's school, Connie's work, their long commutes, and a baby, a new routine had to be established to accommodate juggling all they had to manage.

In addition to all his responsibilities and time commitments, Tymm, upon discharge from active army duty, had signed up for the National Guard. He had his Guard duties to fulfill throughout college and was gone two weekends a month and two weeks each summer for training. It was pre-9/11; the threat of being activated to serve his country as a full-time soldier never crossed his mind. The worst imaginable prospect was helping out during a natural disaster or a riot. A war was unimaginable. Besides, the members of the National Guard hadn't been called to active duty since the Korean War, fifty-five years ago. They weren't even activated during the Vietnam War. Nothing gave Tymm reason to consider life in the National Guard as anything other than a minimal time commitment each year and the chance to assist with a natural disaster once in a blue moon.

Tymm, now a college graduate specializing in curriculum development, began providing full time for his family. He landed a civilian job with the State of Washington's National Guard at Camp Murray in Tacoma, a perfect fit for him. In his soul, he was a military man. But again, he and Connie were presented with a commute problem. Connie wanted to stay with AT&T Wireless; it was an outstanding company to work for, and her job was challenging and fun. Again, they split the distance between them, shortening what was still a long commute for both. Within two and a half years, Emily was introduced to her baby sister, Elizabeth (Lizzy), in 2001. With both of them working full-time jobs, driving long commutes, and raising two young children, life was hectic for this couple. But as they had done with earlier challenges in their marriage, they found ways to make it all work. That's what they did best. They were mastering the art of simplifying chaos.

After the terrorist attacks on September 11 and our nation's subsequent retaliation, Connie and Tymm began to experience heightened concern about their future and the course they had planned. It began with rumors that the National Guard may be called to action. With the shortage of soldiers on the ground in Afghanistan and Iraq, the National Guard, often referred to as "weekend warriors," were poised to take up the slack. The Guard, historically the butt of jokes among the regular U.S. Armed Service personnel for their part-time status, suddenly found their worth as soldiers invaluable. It's been said that there are no atheists in foxholes. In Afghanistan and Iraq, that holds true, and the National Guard mockers had a conversion. They were silent, the "weekend warriors" notion gone. The courageous men and women wearing the National Guard uniforms were, and today still are, held in the highest esteem for the lives they've saved and the goodwill they've fostered. These men and women are no longer considered soft soldiers; they are valued as equal among all soldiers in their contribution to this war. "We were, and are, assigned the highest risk jobs and the worst assignments, proving that the Guardsmen and women are not only up to the tasks but can easily exceed expectations," Washington State National Guard Colonel Phil Dyer exclaims proudly. "We have proven ourselves by our actions."

As the war against terrorists raged on, the Guard began playing a heightened role in its battles. Then, in November of 2003, the call Connie and Tymm had been anticipating came. Tymm was selected to be deployed to Iraq. This time he'd serve in the capacity of a lieutenant, rather than a non-commissioned soldier like he was in the army. He was attached to the 81st Brigade, a composite of 3,800 soldiers, both men and women, from all walks of life.

In Iraq, Tymm would lead a platoon of forty soldiers whose job was to run security patrols in Humvees. Luck of the draw would put a soldier on a Humvee with reinforced armor plating. Tymm was one of the lucky ones. Their assigned mission was to hunt down insurgents (terrorists) before they killed or maimed innocent Iraqis or U.S. personnel. The brave, selfless soldiers running these patrols became the first line of defense in a war unlike any other this nation has ever fought.

What's striking is that the National Guard soldiers and their families were well aware that they lacked the sophisticated body protection, weaponry, and degree of training of their counterparts, and yet they were expected to perform to the same standards. Because they were believed to be inferior by training, many would receive whatever remaining gear was available, much like a younger child wearing the older siblings' clothing. In addition, few military personnel were trained for the type of warfare they would face. But remarkably, the bulk of the National Guard's performance, regardless of what they were asked to do and with or without sophisticated gear, exceeded the expectations of the command.

But what makes the Guard a highly unique group of military men and women is that they spend more years together than their counterparts in other branches of the service. Whereas others may spend months or a couple of years together before relocating to a new assignment, the National Guard post is in your own state, close to your home. Unless they move, the same members show up for duty at the same location. These men and women train and grow in their Guard careers together. They have the opportunity to watch one another's families grow and help each other through good times and bad over the span of as many as twenty years. It's an environment that breeds strong bonds, much like those found in tight-knit families. Trust and loyalty develop not only to those with whom they serve, but to the state that each proudly represents.

As a deployed soldier's wife and a mother of two small children to care for along with her full-time job, Connie's plate was full. The constant worry of having her husband shipped out to the most dangerous region in the world, knowing that this war was different and hearing rumors that the soldiers were not prepared for the battles ahead, was draining on her. Reports in the media of inadequate vehicles, gear, and training for all military personnel to fight this war became a continual burden and worry for Connie. She carried the ever-present fear that the dreaded phone call would come.

Like she had during past challenges in their marriage, Connie sought positive ways to navigate her unsettling but busy days and lonely nights, such as volunteering with the National Guard's Family Services. After all, Connie and Tymm were totally committed to the Guard, whether behind the scenes as a supporting spouse or smack in the middle of daily combat. Serving as a volunteer, Connie had the opportunity to help families cope with a multitude of separation-induced issues, manage their fears, direct them to available resources, and simply listen when a family member needed to talk. Aiding others, she found, took her mind off her own problems and worries; in helping others navigate their own adversities, she discovered renewed strength within herself and tightened her belief that whatever happened, she would make it work.

Connie's energy and unyielding belief that all would work out just the way it was supposed to came from a quiet but deep faith. She'd remind herself, when her burdens were heavy, that her mission was to help those with fewer coping skills or to help those in worse situations than her own. There were many days she had to dig deep inside herself to muster the courage to support others who received the horrific news that their spouse was seriously wounded. Or when the family of such a soldier suffered a breakdown upon hearing that news and experienced a diminished capacity to cope with everyday life. Or the time she received a call to help a soldier who had lost a baby to SIDS. These are tasks no amount of training can ever prepare anyone for. And the sickening thought of Connie being the one to make a call for help was never far from the forefront of her mind.

That dreaded day came. It was August 4, 2004, shortly after Connie returned home from a day at work. Tymm had arrived in Iraq in February, just a few months prior. The caller reported that Tymm had been seriously wounded when an IED (Improvised Explosive Device) blew the front of his armored Humvee off with such force that the vehicle became airborne and crashed back down into the crater formed by the explosion. He had suffered a broken back and facial lacerations from the bomb. All but one soldier survived. The caller also advised her that Tymm was being flown to Germany for surgery to repair the shattered vertebrae in his back. The threat of bone fragments impinging upon his spinal column, paralyzing him if he wasn't so already, made him a priority evacuation. The military's casualty response team would be in touch with further information, he said, before hanging up.

With little else to go on, Connie's head was swimming with "what ifs." In her volunteer work she'd seen and heard a lot. She'd seen bad news turn out good...and she'd seen good news turn out bad. The telephone call was brief, just factual data, which wasn't enough to convince her of Tymm's condition. As potential scenarios about their present and future danced in her head, she held her two little girls tight. With 7,000 miles separating Tymm and Connie, her babies were as close to Tymm as she could get. She was close to family, friends, and the Guard family, yet a sense of aloneness swept over her. No words, no person, could take the feeling away. She needed more information. She needed to see Tymm for herself; she needed to touch him, to hold him. Waiting for the next call was sheer agony.

Finally, at 10:30 that night, the phone rang again, and this time it was Tymm on the line. She was in disbelief at hearing his voice. He was heavily medicated and incoherent but alive and talking, whether it made any sense or not. It was a brief interchange, and it would turn out to be the last contact she'd have for two long days. Connie had no information on Tymm's whereabouts or his condition. All she could do was wait for the military to make contact. She prayed to God that no word, no military personnel standing at her door, was a sign of good news. But she knew the reality: it could also be the opposite. With no information on Tymm, she went through the next days in a fog, going through the motions she had to for her girls. She was now on the receiving end of the Guard's Family Service volunteer work.

Word of Tymm's arrival in Germany came at 3:00 in the morning on the third day after the accident. This time the caller told Connie to prepare to fly to Germany on a 10:00 a.m. flight that same day. Overjoyed that he was now in Germany, and knowing she'd soon be able to see him, lifted her spirits. At the same time, she was overwhelmed by all that had to been done before leaving. Arranging child care for two young children, taking leave from a job, notifying family, and all the other chores requiring attention before leaving for an unknown period of time were daunting tasks with only a seven-hour window until her plane's departure. But consistent with Connie's character, orchestrating these tasks became a welcome diversion from worrying about Tymm. She managed to get it all done and arrived on time for her flight. She was exhausted, but happy at the prospect of seeing her husband in ten hours. With a close family friend caring for the girls, all her focus would be on Tymm and his needs in the coming days and weeks.

Arrival in Germany at the Landstuhl Army Medical Center on August 8 provided confirmation that Tymm would recover. He'd be one of the lucky ones. How he'd recover, however, was unknown. With his vertebrae shattered, surgeons had to take the tiny bone fragments, pack them into a cage, and insert the cage where the vertebrae above and below the shattered one had been fused. In time, the bone fragments would solidify. The healing process would require Tymm to wear a body brace for three months. That he was alive and would be returning home was all the news Connie needed, though.

What surprised Connie was that Tymm looked better than he actually was. His face was cut, including a stitched lip, and he was immobile, but he still looked nothing like she had expected. Having seen her brother's injuries following a horrific auto accident, Tymm looked like he'd run through a briar patch by comparison. But looks were deceiving. Tymm was in excruciating physical anguish. The slightest movement would send searing pain throughout his body, and yet the very fact that he felt that pain was in itself good news—if paralyzed, he wouldn't feel a thing. Although he had a serious injury with an unpredictable recovery ahead of him, the important thing was that he would, indeed, recover.

Tymm, as he lay for hours motionless in his hospital bed in unbearable pain, contemplated his future. Endless questions teased his consciousness. Would he be kicked out of the military? If so, what would he do and when could he work? How were his men in Iraq? Would he walk again? Would he be able to play again with his girls? The bond between he and Connie was impenetrable during health—would it sustain if he was physically impaired? It was easy to say "in sickness and in health" during their marriage vows, but they were both young and healthy then. If he walked again, would he be fit for military duty, a lifelong passion and commitment he desperately wanted to pursue? Although an optimistic man by nature, he was also a realist. He was convincing to others when he'd affirm his belief that a full recovery was in sight, but during his moments alone he'd ponder the possible realities. Not only was his life physically painful right now, but the days following his injury were equally as emotionally and mentally painful. He endured those hours with the knowledge that Connie was with him and that they had support from family and their extended family, the Guard.

Connie, too, was suffering in silence. She'd mastered the art of burying her fears about the future and Tymm's pain, and she kept up her positive attitude while in his presence. Alone at night, though, her tears from worry and exhaustion flowed uncontrollably. Her world had just crashed in around her. Nothing would be the same again, and what life was going to be like now was anyone's guess.

Two and a half weeks later, Connie flew back to the states with Tymm. He was airlifted to Walter Reed Army Medical Center in Bethesda, Maryland. Following overnight hospitalization at Walter Reed, Tymm was again airlifted, but this time back home to Washington State. He was hospitalized at Madigan Army Hospital at Fort Lewis, where he was fitted for a body brace. After receiving his brace, his next step in recovery would be physical therapy.

Tymm was anxious to proceed with his recuperation process. His desire now was to get well, shed the body brace, and return to Iraq with his unit. And, to the astonishment of many, Connie was completely behind his decision and understood his desire to go back. It wasn't that he wanted to leave his family—he didn't. His love for his wife and his little girls was as intense and passionate as any loving husband's or father's would be. Connie wasn't a martyr or a victim of her husband's choices either. They were typical members of a committed National Guard family. "'If you're at risk, I'm not willing to let you stand alone.' That's our commitment to one another in the Guard," Colonel Dyer affirmed to me. Tymm and Connie shared this commitment and were honored and proud to be a part of it. In Tymm's condition, the likelihood of him returning to the war was remote, but he remained optimistic. In order for him to return, he needed to pass a physical to remain in the Guard on active duty. Passing that test became his obsession. First the body brace would have to go; within three months, he had accomplished that. Next was intensive physical therapy. He focused all his energy on committing to a full recovery, hoping that the physical therapy would be his passport back to Iraq.

Connie was back on flexible hours, working from home in order to care for Tymm and the girls. When time permitted, she kept up her volunteering with the National Guard Family Services. This time it was a different Connie helping spouses to cope with loss, injury, and long absences. After her own experience, she had gained a new appreciation for what others endure upon hearing of their loved one having been maimed or killed. She also better understood the heightened concerns and worries about the future. She'd been through it now herself, and the wisdom and understanding she could share with others would provide comfort for many in the future.

After months of grueling physical therapy, Tymm became confident he'd remain in the Guard. Although he pleaded his case of returning to Iraq, he received no assurances. However, within six months of his accident, diligent with his exercises, Tymm passed his physical. Though unable yet to touch his toes, he was still capable of doing most anything required of him in Iraq. His pleas to return had fallen on deaf ears before he had passed his physical; now the surprising results persuaded the decision-makers to let him return. Tymm and Connie were notified that Tymm would return to Iraq and his unit. True to his commitment, he would not let them risk their lives alone. Thrilled beyond words, he'd join his Guard brothers not in the battlefield again, but as the battalion logistics officer.

While many would naturally assume Tymm was selfish or even crazy to return to Iraq with two children and a wife at home after all they'd been through, neither assumption is accurate. Tymm had left behind his other family in Iraq. He was their leader. They'd trained, worked, and lived together—they'd bonded for life. He couldn't and wouldn't desert them. This is the attitude that lies at the core of being part of the National Guard. Tymm did return to his platoon on January 24, 2005, for his unit's two remaining months of deployment. Tymm's mission accomplished, he returned safely back to Washington two months later.

Connie is now finally able to relax. For the moment, there is certainty in her life. She, Tymm, and their daughters are a family united—a family with endurance and courage. A family that is proud to be American.

Author's Observations:

Connie seems to have always known inside herself what was right for her, and she has trusted her gut enough to act on those feelings, even when others disagreed. From an early, unexpected marriage to a plea to complete both her and her husband's education, she always kept her goals in her sight, even while juggling a career, children, and an absent—and later wounded—husband. Through giving of herself through her volunteer work, she maintained a positive perspective on her adversities, continually reminding herself that while the challenges that she faced were hardships indeed, other people were dealing with even greater misfortunes. Standing by her husband's side and supporting his fierce loyalty to his country, Connie's flexibility and perseverance endured, and their relationship is still unified and strong, which she counts among her greatest of blessings.

CHAPTER SEVEN

RUTH

MEET RUTH KIDDER. This remarkable and courageous woman lives in the small rural town of Ashton, Idaho, located on the eastern edge of the state bordering Montana. Ruth grew up living in small farming communities around Idaho as her father moved from farm to farm, working to provide for his family of six children—three girls and three boys. From the time they could walk, the kids were assigned chores and expected to do their share to help by milking cows, feeding chickens, collecting eggs, or baling hay. Age, not gender, determined the degree of difficulty of assigned chores. Ruth's father became her role model and hero. He was a man for whom hard work and adversity were taken in stride as an inescapable part of life. He taught his kids right from wrong, good from bad, a strong work ethic, and coping skills that Ruth would come to desperately need—surprisingly, before she even reached the age of twenty-five.

Maintaining the farm was not only hard work, but also a top priority. The family's very existence depended upon everyone doing whatever it took to provide food. It wasn't unusual to hear of children in their town quitting school to help out at home. Ruth became one of those kids. Finishing school could come later; helping her father was an immediate need for survival. Ruth's formal education would end in the ninth grade. But don't be misled. This very bright and capable woman would soon prove she was equal in the wits and wisdom of those with college degrees.

By nineteen, Ruth found what she thought was her mate for life. Within five years after their marriage, they had three boys—Jared, Christopher, and Michael. Ruth also had something she'd not expected: an alcoholic, abusive husband. After five years of physical and emotional abuse, with paychecks wasted at the bars, Ruth packed up her kids and left. She would manage better on her own without living in fear and fighting for grocery money to feed her children. While waitressing and working odd jobs, Ruth caught the attention of Brian, a man from Ashton that she already knew and liked. Ruth saw Brian every day as he made his stop for lunch after hauling logs out of the forest. His job was hard work; he got up at 2:00 a.m., drove into the mountains, picked up logs, hauled them to town for processing, and then went back again for another load. Nonetheless, even with his hectic schedule, Brian took a keen and invested interest in Ruth, and she in him. After a brief courtship, they were married. Brian embraced her three young boys as if they were his own. He was a good man—responsible, good-natured, and not a drinker. Although the chances of a second marriage succeeding so soon after another had ended were not good, Ruth and Brian defied the odds on many levels as their life together unfolded.

As Jared, the oldest of the three boys, entered kindergarten, the family doctor told Ruth that Jared's clumsiness when running was because he was knock-kneed. Ruth and Brian thought nothing of it. If that's what the doctor said, it must be so. Taking the doctor's word for it, Jared entered school but complained about not being able to run and keep up with the other kids. As the months passed, it became apparent that his difficulties were worsening. Then his younger brother, four-year-old Chris, began to show similar symptoms. Going on a mother's instinct, Ruth took the boys to Idaho Falls, the nearest large city, for a second opinion. It was this trip that would turn Ruth and Brian's lives upside down.

After a brief exam, the physician informed them that both Jared and Chris had muscular dystrophy (MD). To Ruth's horror, Michael, her youngest son, had his blood tested and was also found to have the same condition. All three of her boys were afflicted with the deadliest, cruelest form of MD possible. Compounding the devastation of the news that none of her children would live to see their twentieth birthdays, Ruth was twelve-weeks pregnant with a potentially afflicted fourth child. How, she asked, could this be happening? No one in her family or the boys' biological family that she knew of had the disease. Something was terribly wrong, and it led back to Ruth, who was discovered to carry the single aberrant gene.

Upon learning that Ruth was the carrier of the mutant gene and was also pregnant, the doctors encouraged her to have her unborn baby checked. If the baby was diagnosed with MD, they advised her, she could abort. With the prognosis that they'd all have had tracheotomies, breathe on respirators, and be in wheelchairs by grade school, managing three children with MD would be a full-time job twenty-four hours a day, seven days a week, for however many years they made it through. Adding a fourth afflicted child would be virtually impossible for Ruth and Brian to handle. But abortion was unfathomable to them, and "impossible" was never a word Ruth and Brian accepted, no matter how difficult or trying their circumstances. The decision was a clear one for them: Ruth would carry the child to term without the test. It made no difference whether the baby had MD or not. Regardless, they'd love and care for it.

With the despairing news of all three children's bleak futures and the burdens they'd bear so young, Ruth went into denial. "What mother wouldn't? Imagine being told that the dreams you have for your children and the questions you have about their lives are pointless. Questions like, which sports will they play? How will they look when they graduate from high school? What colleges will they attend? What careers will they choose? Who will they marry? How many children will they have? Imagine thinking about the joy, the laughter, the football and baseball games at school and in the back yard, the frogs and critters stuffed into their pockets as trophies from prowling around in the woods..." These are the thoughts and memories stored before the events even happen. Imagine losing it all in one moment of one day. Your precious children have so much life and happiness intended for them, but you're told none of what you thought or planned for them will ever happen. Their future will be not only short, but also miserable. They will be confined first to wheelchairs, then to beds, immobile, unable to breathe on their own because their diaphragms will be the first organs to shut down. How does a mother even begin to comprehend the magnitude of that reality?

Ruth heard the words, but couldn't make sense of them in her mind. Her whole being rejected the diagnosis. She could speak the doctor's verdict and fill buckets with her tears, but deep in her soul she fought it intensely. She fought it so much that she ignored the doctor's orders to get all three boys into a vigorous exercise regime with a therapist. She couldn't do it. If she did, she'd be admitting that she was on the verge of losing her children. And she knew the odds were stacked against her unborn, innocent child that she and Brian had so much love for already. Accepting three boys with MD meant she'd have to accept the probability that her fourth child would suffer the same fate. It was all too much to absorb. She'd been raised to deal with tough times, but this was beyond anything she could have imagined. And the pinnacle of her spiral of grief was that it was her gene that had caused this to happen. Ruth was swimming in a sea of guilt.

Admittedly, there was another added component to Ruth's feelings of culpability: her guilt over understandably thinking about the impact this news would have on her own life. Every moment of every day was going to be spent caring for invalid and completely dependent children. This was not how she had envisioned her life to be. No vacations, no family outings, no idle hours spent in town, no frills, no second income to enjoy meals out, no new clothes...the list went on. Ruth's guilt intensified each time she thought of herself and the losses she'd have to endure. She was only in her mid-twenties—a young adult faced with burdens beyond her years.

Wracked with guilt and gripped by fear, her safe haven—her coping mechanism—was her denial. Denial allowed Ruth the ability to function with some normalcy. And it worked, until one fateful day. It was six months after she first heard those horrific words: all three boys, and most likely your unborn baby, will die by their teenage years. Reality came to Ruth in the form of an occupational therapist. She sat Ruth down and didn't mince words. She told Ruth that she'd have to accept the facts and start doing what she could to help her children. "It's no longer about you. It's about them. They need you to do what is right for them. Now is the time. Later is too late. It's up to you to give them the best quality of life this dreadful disease will afford them. Save you for later; it's about your children now."

Whether it was how she said it or the words she used, the therapist shook Ruth out of her malaise. From that day forward, denial was replaced by the grit and tenacity with which her father had raised her. And it was the same grit and tenacity that Brian had. He stood by her side every inch of the way. He was working hard to support the family and pay the mounting medical bills of his stepsons. His love was not merely words; he was there for his family, the family he made a commitment to when he said "I do, in sickness and in health." Whatever crosses Ruth and Brian had to bear, they'd bear them together. There was too much work ahead of them to waste time and energy on guilt for something that was no one's fault. If this was God's plan, then God would give them the strength and the knowledge to care for their children.

But God wasn't always revered. In fact, there were many months at first when the only communication with God that Ruth could muster was to question how He could have allowed this to happen to her boys and to her and Brian. It was cruel and unforgivable. How could a loving God take the lives of their children? Was there even a God? Ruth angrily asked many times throughout the day, what have I done to deserve this? What have four innocent little boys done to deserve a slow death by first taking their mobility, then the very muscles they need to breathe air, and then incapacitating them one muscle at a time? Why, God? Why would you do this to them? It wasn't until their pastor, Pastor Laux, took them under his wing that this desperate family found someone to help them make sense of a seemingly senseless situation.

Pastor Laux gave them back the gift of faith. He enabled them to see their world through a different set of lenses. "What if this happened to be a blessing and not a curse? What if you did nothing to deserve this, but instead you were the right mother and father to care for these children, these gifts from God? What if He put them in your care for safekeeping here on earth? What if He put Brian in Ruth's life to love and cherish not only her but also her boys? Why is it that your marriage is flourishing and not disintegrating with these challenges as so many others do?"

A different set of questions opened their hearts to a new beginning. A determination and commitment took root in their souls to make their own lives and those of their boys the best lives possible. That there was no money for assistance didn't matter. That neither Ruth nor Brian had the educational background or contacts to navigate the maze of the medical community and the resourceful government agencies didn't matter either. If they had to, they'd go it alone; they would figure it out along the way. With their original hopes and dreams for each of their boys' lives extinguished, they decided to create new ones for the years they'd be given.

Within the first year of his diagnosis, Jared became confined to a wheelchair. He still wanted to live as regular a life as possible, however, and that started with remaining in school. With Chris right behind him, within two years both boys were wheelchair-bound but still in school. Ruth wanted to hold onto that one shred of normalcy for them, and the boys wanted it too. Learning wasn't a problem, but their teacher's ability to manage children with physical disabilities was. The teachers were trained to work with mentally challenged, not physically challenged, kids. As a result, Ruth was back and forth from home to school constantly. She also had to feel the additional burden and heartache a parent experiences when they know their children are being teased by other kids.

Ruth finally reached a breaking point. No longer able to deal with the pain of knowing her children were being mocked unmercifully, she decided to homeschool them. Ruth, a high school dropout, was so committed to her mission of giving her children the best life possible that she took on the role of teacher. After Ruth made her decision to protect her boys from humiliation at school, she was told by a school social worker that removing the kids from school would be bad for them. She lectured Ruth on how they needed the socialization that school provided. Undaunted by this so-called educated expert on what was best for her kids, Ruth could not fathom how ridicule could be considered healthy socialization. If well-honed socialization skills were beneficial to children, Ruth couldn't help but wonder why the school wasn't focusing their energies on teaching kids how to socialize appropriately with the mentally and physically disabled. She stood her ground and realigned her busy days to accommodate being a teacher as well.

Even with Brian at her side, Ruth often experienced intense feelings of isolation. As the feelings of aloneness persisted, Ruth was befriended by an ostensible angel, Ruth Clark. Ruth and her husband also had four boys and were living in Rexburg, Idaho, not too far away. Although the Clark boys had Becker's muscular dystrophy, a type of MD that affords a normal life span, their mother Ruth was still a comfort and a hero to Ruth, Brian, and the boys. On the especially bad days, when despairing news about the boys' health or just plain old exhaustion caused the self-pity and fear to creep back in, Ruth Clark's support and friendship would ease Ruth's emotional pain and ready her for the weeks and months ahead.

By third grade, Michael, her third son, was confined to a wheelchair. And by the age of ten, her youngest son, Jess, was forced into a wheelchair as well, having not been able to escape inheriting the horrific disease. With no medical insurance to help, footing the bills alone was becoming increasingly difficult. Yet Ruth held onto her solo care, believing that no one could care for her boys like their own mother. But the toll this hardship was taking on her was heavy, and the signs that she could no longer go it alone were glaring. Courageous though she was, if she didn't take care of herself, she couldn't be there for her children. Finally, she surrendered and reached out for help.

Ruth and Brian applied for and were granted Medicaid and Social Security. Ruth now had aides part time to help with the boys, and most of their expense was covered. The remainder they paid out-of-pocket, as they continue to do to this day. It was worth every penny. Without the extraordinary nurses and aides to lend a hand, Ruth would not have been able to keep the boys at home. These very special people gave of themselves a gift unmatched.

By June of 1999, Jared, the eldest at eighteen years of age, lost his battle to breathe and slipped away. Losing her firstborn son was devastating. "Just because you know it will happen, that doesn't make death and losing a child any easier," she explains. "It felt like someone ripped my heart out." I heard the pain and the ache in her heart as she shared these words with me.

Then on November 1, 2002, another devastating blow hit the Kidder family. Just five days shy of his sixteenth birthday, Ruth and Brian's only son together, Jess, contracted pneumonia and unexpectedly died. The fact that he was a fighter from the get-go and had suffered fewer years than his brothers made it a tough loss to accept. The devastation of a mother, father, and two remaining brothers, both of whom were bedridden, intubated, and on ventilators, was unfathomable. And yet, even with Chris and Michael's clutches on life as tenuous as they were, the very fact that these other two sons continued to live gave Ruth and Brian the strength to go on.

The tenacity that Ruth, Brian, Michael, and Chris demonstrate each and every day is beyond comprehension. Today, Michael and Chris have outlived the medical experts' predictions. Both boys are becoming highly skilled specialized computer users. With the help of professional craftsmen, Brian had the outside wall to the boys' bedroom hinged so that it can lift up, opening the entire room to the outside. Now on warm and sunny days, their beds and ventilators are wheeled outside on the back porch where they can watch the dog play, the squirrels scamper across the yard, and the birds sing on the branches hanging above.

On Sundays, Pastor Laux comes to the Kidder home and performs a special service for the family. God is no longer chastised for His unfairness, but is instead an integral daily part of the Kidder household. With their strong faith, their deeply committed love, and their extended family and close friends, this home is flourishing. They have navigated every adversity with courage and determination and with a deep and profound love for their children and each other. Nothing has stopped them from doing all they can for their boys. And Brian still gets up at 2:00 in the morning to make his twice-daily trip deep into the forest of eastern Idaho to pick up a load of logs to haul back to town. On good days, when help back at home is available, Ruth's special treat is not a cruise in the Caribbean aboard a luxury liner or a fancy new car, but instead a cruise into town to join Brian for lunch before he heads back to the woods. All they long for in their lives is a cure for MD. That's their concept of success: finding a cure that will give their two remaining boys life and save other children and parents from the heartache of this terrible disease.

And Ruth, when not attending to her boys or having a special lunch date with Brian, is studying for her G.E.D. Someday, she says, she'll have the education to become a children's advocate—to be a voice where there is none. No one should have to have a state representative visit their home because their child has been denied funding for a tracheotomy and ventilator. "I want to fight for kids. That's my dream," she says with a spirit of hope and love. She claims that she throws an occasional pity party, but I never heard a hint of one. I heard no self-pity, no anger, and no resentment. All I heard is a mother deeply in love with her husband and her boys and happy with her faith, her friends, her family, and the support of her community. Ask her who she looks up to—who her heroes are—and she'll beam with pride at the answer: "Jared, Chris, Michael, and Jess are and always will be. I'm blessed to be their mother."

Author's Observations:

Few can imagine the devastation a young mother feels when given the news that most likely all of her children will die before they reach their twentieth birthdays. But Ruth courageously navigated her way through the storm of emotions that followed. In a matter of seconds, Ruth lost her grip on reality, but she eventually managed to shake off her denial and pull herself up for the sake of her boys. In time, she began to see her dire circumstances in a new way. She turned her anger toward God into gratitude for believing in her strength enough to give her such an enormous challenge to face. She cherished the "little things" in her life, like watching her two ill sons enjoy the outdoors from the confines of their hospital beds and spending some precious moments alone with her husband. Ruth discovered that her endurance, her unconditional love for her husband and sons, and her devotion to each of her boys are the true gifts from God.

CHAPTER EIGHT

AYSEL

MEET AYSEL KURDA SANDERSON. Nothing about this woman would lead you to believe that life for her was anything but easy. She is a proud mother of a twelve-year-old and an accomplished plastic and reconstructive surgeon, specializing in cosmetic surgery. Her demeanor is soft-spoken, and her outward appearance transforms from nondescript to classy depending upon her daily activities. Most often, she is wearing hospital scrubs, and if it weren't for her physician nameplate, she could be taken for anyone working in a medical setting. She's unpretentious and down-to-earth, with no hint of arrogance or superiority. She's easy to like—and just as easy to misread.

As a surgeon, she has high standards for herself and her staff. There are no excuses for not giving each patient the very best in surgical skill, care, and attention. Aysel's standards are not compromised, and her loyal patient following along with new referrals keeps her booked for consultations and surgeries months in advance. She has no need for costly advertising; she is a patient-driven surgeon. What many busy physicians delegate to their nursing staff, Aysel does herself, costing her time and money but paying off in patient as well as personal satisfaction. These tasks include listening to patients to fully understand their needs and expectations. "I learn from my patients when I take the time to listen carefully. If I rush them, I might miss something important, something I need to know that will give my patients optimum results," Aysel explains. She has made it one of her trademarks to understand the whole person—both physically and emotionally—behind the physical patient. It's not uncommon for patients to believe that fixing something on the outside will in turn fix something on the inside. If Aysel doesn't understand a patient's motivation and intent, she may not be able to achieve his or her desired outcome, which is what success as a cosmetic surgeon is all about.

Long before becoming a surgeon entered her mind, she was still enjoying innocence as a seven-year-old child when her parents informed her that they were moving. But they weren't moving across town or even across the country. They were moving across the Atlantic Ocean, leaving their native Turkey for the United States. America was known then, just as it is now, to be the land of opportunity, and Aysel's family was no different from other immigrants hungry for the chance to participate in the American dream. Her father, H. Kurda, had been born in Crimea, Russia. He escaped during WWII and eventually made his way to Turkey, where he met and married Aysel's mother in Ankara, the capital city. They agreed they'd start their family in Turkey, but their dream to go to America was never far from their thoughts. Known for their determination, they were committed to turning that dream into a reality. So with two girls in tow (Aysel, seven, and her younger sister Sevinc, "Susan", two), their parents packed what they could cram into three suitcases and left all that was familiar to them behind. Their mother and father went through this life-altering change in order to guarantee a better life for their daughters. They vowed to stay in the U.S. for five years before they would return to their native homeland.

On November 22, 1963, the day President John F. Kennedy was shot and killed, the Kurdas landed in New York. The Kurdas didn't understand a word of English and therefore had no idea why passengers and airport staff were holding loved ones close and shedding tears. They also didn't understand the significance of the moment of silence on the airplane prior to deplaning. With chaos and confusion surrounding them, the Kurdas navigated their way out of the airport terminal to their awaiting ride. It wasn't until they were among bilingual old friends that the origin of the confusion came to light. The country they planned to call home for the next five years was under heightened vigilance in case the president's assassination was just the beginning of a planned attack on America. Although they weren't U.S. citizens, the Kurdas still felt the hollowing depth of the country's tragedy. They were even introduced to television for the first time while watching JFK's funeral, and they too shed tears for the lost president.

The first stop for the Kurda family was Queens, a borough of New York City. They moved in temporarily with a couple who opened their one-bedroom apartment to them, until Mr. Kurda (originally a diesel mechanic by trade) found a job as the maintenance man of an apartment building in Far Rockaway. By the new year, Aysel was enrolled in school. She was immediately put back a grade due to her inability to speak and understand English. But after a month in first grade, with the help of after-school tutoring, Aysel advanced to second grade, the grade she had been in when she had left Turkey. After two years in Far Rockaway, the family moved to Cedarhurst on Long Island, New York, where Mr. Kurda had found a better job as the custodian for a Jewish Sephardic Temple. The job was even more helpful because the family was able to live in a small apartment within the temple, which allowed them to save money for Mr. Kurda's medallion that he needed in order to own and operate a taxicab. He was able to attain that objective within only a few short years.

With his family settled in America, Mr. Kurda pursued his career as a cab driver while Aysel completed her elementary and high school years in Cedarhurst. By this time, it was evident that Mr. and Mrs. Kurda were here to stay. Five years had come and gone, and instead of preparing to leave the U.S., they were putting down roots. Citizenship was their ultimate goal.

Aysel, meanwhile, was excelling in her studies, taking advanced classes in math and science throughout junior high and high school. Her group of friends was composed of classmates from her school on weekdays and Crimean Turks from the Turkish community on weekends. As a young immigrant acutely taking note of the different environments and attitudes around her, she made an observation and a decision that would greatly impact her future. Aysel found that her aspirations of attending an Ivy League university and becoming a professional of some sort were not consistent with the goals of the other Crimean Turkish kids, who were focused primarily on attending community colleges. Amid this polarity, Aysel learned that she could pick and choose the favorable elements of both cultures and communities, thereby having the best of both worlds. She was nurtured and stayed connected to her cultural roots within the Turkish community, but received her educational mandates from her school friends' parents. She applied to and was accepted at Cornell University, one of our nation's most prestigious universities. She became the first child in the Crimean Turkish community to attend an Ivy League university. Aysel later learned that she had raised the bar, setting a new standard for her community and its youth.

With her dad's limited income as a cab driver, Aysel had to earn her way through college. She took out student loans and received a partial scholarship for the first year; what that didn't cover she paid for herself in an exhausting variety of different jobs over her time at Cornell. She worked as a short-order cook in the dining hall, a research assistant in the veterinary school, a research assistant in the microbiology lab more than thirty hours a week, a night auditor, a front desk receptionist at two hotels, and a waitress during the summer, along with participating in the work-study financial aid program. Of course, this was all while taking a full class load at Cornell, not exactly an easy task in and of itself. Aysel was living proof to each and every young immigrant that the American dream could truly be a reality—if you were willing to work hard enough.

As a student at Cornell, Aysel majored in microbiology. By graduation, she had met and later married her husband and they soon moved to Dallas, where her husband had accepted a position. She waitressed for a few months before accepting a position with the University of Texas Southwestern Medical Center as a research assistant. After more than a year of suffering through tedious, lonely hours each day, performing the same experiments over and over again, Aysel decided that life as a lab tech wasn't for her. However, jobs were limited without a graduate degree. She decided to change her career course and become a physician.

Aysel applied to and was accepted at the University of Texas Medical Branch at Galveston. She and her husband moved to Webster, Texas, between Houston, where her husband was able to be transferred within his company, and Galveston, where Aysel started medical school. Although her husband was gainfully employed at this point, Aysel wanted to contribute what she could to their income. Even though she was a full-time student, she began working part-time at a local hospital writing up histories and performing physicals for attending physicians.

By her fourth year of medical school, Aysel had discovered that her passion in medicine was surgery. She applied and was accepted to do her internship at the University of Maryland Medical Center. She went on to complete her four-year surgical residency there as well, working on-call for Bethlehem Steel in their clinic when not working at the hospital.

Unbeknownst to Aysel, she would soon face an even greater challenge than financial woes within the world of surgery: enduring the ordeals of being a woman within a male-dominated environment. Although women are entering the medical profession at an ever-increasing rate and have earned their acceptance in internal medicine, surgeons—mostly men—are a different breed from their counterparts. Surgery has always been seen as a man's specialty. If a woman is to survive her surgical residency, she needs to be tough, courageous, totally committed, and "one of the boys." She also needs to prove herself very quickly. For Aysel in Maryland, all surgical internships and residencies were based on a pyramid program, wherein a given number of residents were cut from the program each year and only a few remained for the final chief residency in the fifth year.

Once again, Aysel had to do what others weren't willing to in order to achieve her goal. Her residency required her to become a stand-out resident surgeon and unequivocally demonstrate that her skills and abilities were equal to—or even greater than—her fellow male residents. She endured verbal sexual innuendos, coped with strong male egos, and dealt with teasing and mockery. She and her skills were under a microscope at all times. Any flaws would be magnified because she was a woman.

However, Aysel was strong and committed. She didn't ask for or demand respect—she earned it. She proved that women are just as capable as men of becoming first-class surgeons. She kept her eyes, mind, and heart focused on her goal. She decided that she had two choices: to be miserable or to find ways to deal effectively with her situation and save her energy for mastering her skills. She chose the latter. She also did what many female surgical residents didn't do: she maintained her femininity and did not allow herself to be transformed into a rough-and-tough female in order to fit in and be accepted.

Having observed firsthand what a surgical residency could turn females into, Aysel made a promise to herself. She would not become arrogant or conceited and would always treat all people with respect, dignity, and equality. She would not let her ego control her or her attitude toward colleagues, patients, or her staff. Even now, when she's mistaken for a nurse or a visitor, Aysel is unflustered. She smiles and moves on, or, if necessary, makes a polite correction that she's a surgeon. She knows that being a physician is what she does, and not who she is.

By the end of her surgical residency, Aysel had decided on her specialty: plastic and reconstructive surgery. It was a discipline in which the science of medicine and her creativity would work in unison to provide the best patient outcomes and highest personal gratification. She went on to attend the Medical College of Virginia, and after two years of understudy from some of the nation's most highly skilled plastic and reconstructive surgeons, Aysel K. Sanderson, M.D. was ready to begin her private practice. With her formal learning behind her, Aysel believed that her subjection to sexist stereotypes was behind her as well. Unfortunately, she'd face it again years later in a very different context, much to her disbelief. But for now, she'd achieved her goal in spite of the uphill battle. She was ready to show patients there was a kinder, gentler surgeon in town.

It was time to find a location, set up practice, treat patients, and enjoy the fruits of many years of hard work and education. Her husband, originally from California, wanted to return to the West Coast—this time to the Seattle area. Again, another big career decision was upon Aysel. She had to decide whether to join an existing surgical practice or start her own. After arriving in Seattle and seeing what was available, she learned of a plastic surgeon who had abruptly lost his life. His practice was for sale and it seemed to be a perfect fit. The office was a turnkey practice; if she bought it, complete with a willing staff and an accompanying operating room, she could start practicing immediately. Her office search ended, and she negotiated the sale, moved west, and started her practice in August of 1991.

The American dream was alive and well in Aysel, who had spent almost half of her life working and educating herself to take advantage of the vast opportunities possible in the United States. Aysel was now a proud American surgeon, fulfilling her and her parents' dream. "Five years" was over long ago; the entire Kurda family was here to stay. America actually was all it was cracked up to be as long as you worked hard, took nothing for granted, and earned your keep. Like it had been for so many immigrants before the Kurdas, nothing seemed out of reach.

There was one cultural norm—both Turkish and American—that Aysel had not yet managed to comply with: becoming a mother. Although her parents were immensely proud of their eldest daughter's achievements, they began urging her to have a child. They wanted Aysel to experience the joys of parenthood in her lifetime. She had left a legacy of academic achievement; now it was time to leave a legacy of a child. They even offered to relocate from New York to Seattle to care for the baby when it arrived, allowing Aysel to continue to work. Aysel did want children eventually, but she was committed to getting her practice off the ground first.

With her new practice open for patients, Aysel began to make herself known within the medical community. She didn't do it through self-promotion like many do, but instead through her skills as a surgeon and her determination to change the dynamics of the doctor/patient relationship. She wanted to set the example for how such a relationship should be, and she was confident that others would surely follow. Her formal education transitioned into a continuing informal education by her patients. She asked questions, listened with the intent to fully understand, resisted the pressure to rush, and demonstrated to patients that they were her highest priority. Dedicated to staying focused and not underestimating patients' needs, she built an enviable practice and earned the respect and admiration of her colleagues. From her earliest years, Aysel was taught to treat all individuals in the same way she would want to be treated herself. She continues to follow this lesson in her professional life in the same way she does in her personal life.

Due to her thriving practice, Aysel became the first woman, as well as the youngest physician, to ever hold the esteemed position of chief of surgery at Overlake Hospital Medical Center in Bellevue, Washington. She also served for several years as head of the Credentialing Board, which provides physician oversight. In addition, her colleagues asked her to stay on another year as the first female president of the Washington Society of Plastic and Reconstructive Surgeons because of her ability to bring people together for the common good.

In her third year of private practice, Aysel discovered she was pregnant. True to their word, her parents relocated and came to live with Aysel and her husband. Her son was born in 1994, and her home was remodeled so her parents could live comfortably in their own space, separate and apart from the main house. When Aysel was at work, her parents cared for their grandson; when she wasn't working, she was a full-time mother, loving every minute of it.

What has been left unmentioned until now is the fact that Aysel emigrated from a Muslim country and was raised as a Muslim. Being a Muslim had never been a stigma or an issue before. The Kurdas taught their girls that their faith was a peaceful and morally accountable religion. They were also taught not to distinguish between "good and bad" people based upon their religious beliefs; actions and attitudes, not religion, distinguished one's character. But on September 11, 2001, Aysel received a wake-up call that narrow-minded, uninformed Americans would now paint all Muslims with the same large, prejudicial brush. The fundamental premise of the Muslim faith, as Aysel and her sister were taught in Turkey, was the opposite of what the terrorists did in the name of their faith. The basic tenets of Islamic faith—being helpful, kind, and loving—are the same values that are taught to any God-loving, religious American. The trauma inflicted upon this country on 9/11 was devastating to good people of all faiths, American Muslims like Aysel included.

Moving on after the country's tragedy, with a healthy son and a successful career, Aysel's life seemed to be perfect. But all was not as it appeared. Her marriage was falling apart. By 2003, it was obvious there was no viable solution to the many complex issues that led to its demise. During the course of the divorce proceedings, sexism reared its ugly head once again. This time, however, it proved to be far crueler than anything that was said or done in an operating room. Her husband, who had been unemployed for years after being laid off, could represent himself as a "stay-at-home dad" and seek full custody. Aysel's mothering abilities were called into question. After all, it was asked, how could a practicing surgeon have custody of a child, with or without her parents living in the home? Aysel needed to prove that she could be a good mother and a good surgeon.

Devastated and in shock upon learning that the courts could very well rule against her, she pulled herself together. This would be no different than all the other times she'd had to prove herself. She would do what she had to rather than standing idly by and becoming a victim of injustice. In her heart, she knew that if the circumstances were reversed and a man was in her position, he'd prevail. His profession would not be a determining factor as to whether or not he was a capable father. Determined and devoted to her son, she prevailed. Rather than trying to prove that busy working women could do it all (and to spare her son from a painfully drawn-out divorce process), Aysel cut back her practice hours instead, substantially reducing her income but managing to keep custody. She missed practicing full time, but soon discovered the joy of spending more time with her son, something she'd regretted missing out on before. The outcome of the divorce and Aysel's decision benefited both her and her son.

With the divorce behind her and her son flourishing, Aysel's life was back on track. But as often happens, adversity strikes when we least expect it. Aysel's father was diagnosed with Alzheimer's disease, and shortly thereafter her mother was found to have a multitude of medical problems as well, including mild senile dementia. Being their primary care provider has taken its emotional toll on Aysel. Slowly losing her parents through their inability to communicate is painful beyond words. The two people who have lovingly sacrificed so much for her and that she has been so dependent upon are now totally dependent upon her. Now she not only has her patients and her son to care for, but now her ill parents as well. And financially, she has her practice's ongoing overhead, her ex-husband's monthly allotment, and her parents' medical bills, not to mention her and her son's own living expenses. The burdens are substantial, but her will is even greater. Her love has no conditions, no boundaries. She embraces the fact that she is able to give something back to them and keep them with her at home for as long as possible...hopefully through their last days. Sure it's hard on her, but she wouldn't dream of doing anything differently. She's in it for the long haul. She knows she has the strength and the capacity to keep going—for her parents and for herself.

Today, when new surgeons come to town, it's not uncommon to hear that the "go to" person for help in establishing a practice is none other than Aysel. She's never seen competition as a threat, but rather as an opportunity to mentor, coach, and help new colleagues get started. She is secure in her reputation as one of the most highly skilled surgeons in the area and has nurtured a loyal patient and physician following who are generous with and confident in their referrals.

Without the influence of this determined and brave woman who overcame so many adversities, there'd be fewer educated Turks, fewer patient-driven surgeons, fewer happy patients, and one less person to lead the way for other fledgling surgeons, demonstrating that unconditional love is still a treasured value. From being an immigrant, to becoming a surgeon and a mother, to taking on the care of her ailing parents, to practicing her Muslim faith with confidence and pride, Aysel has proven that there is no adversity so great that it can't be overcome with courage, conviction, hard work, and belief in oneself. Her motto: "Where there's a will, there's a way, even though it may not be so easy.".

     🌿   🌿   🌿

Author's Observations:

With all the excuses in the world to settle into mediocrity, Aysel, from a young age, learned to skillfully observe and make conscious decisions to capitalize on the American dream. Her foreign background, her gender, and her parents' lack of financial resources were never deterrents. Her refusal to become a victim and her determination to hold onto her dignity and self-respect when confronted with sexism can set an example for all women faced with similar circumstances. The love she had for—and from—her family and friends sustained her throughout the most difficult times. Her commitment to her son, her parents, and her patients gives her the energy and the will to manage her many burdens with grace and ease. Some would think that because she is a physician, she has it made. But it is because of who she is and how she behaves that she has succeeded. She continues to navigate each adversity with courage and a passion for doing the right thing, just as she has always done. In doing so, Aysel has set new, higher standards for adhering to the values inherent in family and work.

CHAPTER NINE

MARY NELLA

MEET MARY NELLA McLAUGHLIN. She's a selfless, focused, and enthusiastic participant in life. Her accomplishments at age fifty-eight are already too numerous to list—and she still has a lot of life left in her. Her life has been anything but normal. In fact, Mary Nella has been an ordained minister since the early 1980s, when it was difficult for a woman to work in what had historically been regarded as a man's vocation. But Mary Nella has a history of going against the tide, forging ahead and proving she's capable of doing pretty much anything imaginable.

At the young age of five, Mary Nella and her brother were harshly introduced to the realization that life can be massively unfair. Her father, the man she idolized, was permanently institutionalized with mental disabilities, rendering him incapable of coping with the responsibilities of work and a family. Focused on her own acting career and sustaining the family, their self-absorbed mother left Mary Nella and her brother with their grandparents, sending money from the odd jobs she worked to sustain herself while waiting for her big break. In essence, they lost both their parents at the same time. But as grandparents often do, they became instrumental in building character and drive in both of the children's lives. They gave each a solid moral and spiritual foundation from which to grow into productive, responsible adults. In most all respects, Mary Nella and her brother were better off with their grandparents than they would have been if they'd remained under their mother's care.

That being said, losing their mother to her career was not easy for two children to accept. Although their grandparents loved them, the permanent absence of their father and the prolonged absences of their mother left emotional scars and conflicts. For Mary Nella, she longed for her father's touch, his lap to sit on, and his constant reminders of his love for her. But the fact that he was sick and in a hospital was easier for the children to accept than their mother's abandonment to fulfill her own ambitions.

Mary Nella, unlike her brother, dealt with her anger and confusion not by excelling but by dropping out of school. She spent her late teens and early twenties looking for thrills and adventure. For thrills, she indulged in alcohol and drugs. For adventure, she headed to Mexico, where she hung out with other kids struggling with their own internal conflicts. In time, life in Mexico got boring, so Mary Nella devised a new plan. She'd head back to California, but not to her grandparents' home. She would move in with her mother in the hopes of finding the maternal presence she longed for. Her escape south of the border had initially dulled her emotional pain, but it returned with a vengeance once the fun wore off. Confident her mother would be all that she longed for—mature and remorseful and longing for a chance to prove her love—Mary Nella happily left her friends for a more fulfilling life.

Her visions of all things wonderful between mother and daughter, however, were not to be. Mary Nella learned the heartbreakingly hard way that she couldn't help her mother if her mother wasn't willing to help herself. With her dreams of a healthy relationship with her mother up in smoke, Mary Nella left, undecided about her future.

During a visit from one of her cousins, Mary Nella talked to her about her inner struggles and the emotional pain she was undergoing from the realization that her mother was not going to be there for her. She also confessed that she had felt so hopeless, confused, and miserable, her inability to focus on her high goals, that she had attempted suicide twice. She tried alcohol and drugs to dull the pain, but to no avail. Her cousin suggested that she pray and seek the Lord's guidance for her future. Mary Nella had tried other solutions, all self-defeating and resulting in nothing. So, although she didn't think it would help, she agreed to try it, figuring it couldn't hurt. Before she prayed, her cousin confronted her with how she was living her life in an attempt to open her mind and be receptive to God. On her knees, her cousin prayed, "Jesus, would you come into Mary Nella's life and heart? She has lost control and needs your help."

Within moments, Mary Nella had a powerful physical transformation. Her tears dried and a warmth she'd never experienced before enveloped her, peace permeating her body to the bones. The desperation, fear, confusion, and hopelessness were gone. In their place was a sense of hope, for the first time in fifteen years. Life was worth living again. In addition to prayer, Mary Nella returned to the invaluable lessons learned from her grandparents. She had been taught to have goals, to be productive, to be of good character, to not shirk responsibilities, and to be a leader. Through prayer and a return to her roots, hope for a meaningful life flooded through her, filling her spirit with a surge in energy she had not experienced before. She began to chart a new course with determination. Her brother had a radio show in Los Angeles, and after a short stint working for him, she started a Christian radio and publishing company. Furthermore, the surreal religious experience she'd undergone led her to what would be her life's passion and vocation. She entered a local seminary.

In a conservative seminary, Mary Nella made the unhappy discovery that women were not taken seriously unless their ambition was to be a helpmate, a pastor's wife, or a children's worker. They were not predicted to hold leadership roles. Disappointed and dejected, she left seminary before becoming ordained. However, she still embraced her unshakable faith in Christianity. Shortly after her departure from seminary, Mary Nella met, fell in love with, and married David, who also worked in Christian media. After several years, their pastor suggested that Mary Nella, now thirty-five with three children, go back to seminary and become ordained. He convinced her that things would be different now at seminary, so she and David readily took his advice. They both enrolled in seminary in Chicago, where they became ordained ministers.

Mary Nella and David were called to pastor a church in South Chicago in a declining neighborhood with all the urban problems of gangs, abuse, and homelessness. They decided to dedicate their preaching lives to ministering to and serving the poor and homeless. Their rationale for moving into a run-down neighborhood with three children was simple: it was the only way to really learn about the community's members. Living, working, and raising children within the environment would give them firsthand knowledge of how best to help them. It didn't take long for this altruistic couple to discover they were not equipped to deal with the homeless or the abused population. Volunteering at the food bank was one thing; living amongst the most desperate of our society was entirely different. But with the conviction that there was a reason they were called to pastor a church in the midst of urban poverty, they committed to stay the course.

Mary Nella and David began to work with the church's leadership and other churches and community organizations to find a way to alleviate the suffering all around them. They knew the problems were larger than their church could successfully take on. Rather than shrugging their shoulders in a sea of hopelessness, they instead founded a nonprofit organization named the Barnabas Project. Their first objective was to buy a house, with the local bank's financing assistance, for the homeless families in their church. The families' contribution would be their sweat equity in fixing it up and keeping it in good repair. This house would be known as the Jubilee House.

Their second project was developing an apartment building called Wellspring, designed to be a transitional living facility for homeless and abused women with children. It flourished by giving these women a chance to get on their feet and work their way towards independence. Wellspring is still in existence today.

As often happens, the thrill of victory—in this case two ambitious concepts turned into successful realities—led to the quest for more victories. Not ones to sit back and applaud themselves, Mary Nella and David got busy with a third project. This time they partnered with Jesus People, an inner-city ministry, and bought a high-rise apartment building, the Leland House, to provide shelter for homeless families with children, which is still run today by the Barnabas Project.

By now, Mary Nella had gained a reputation as a collaborator. Having no money of her own, ideas and outcomes were dependent upon joining forces with those who did. Her wit and wisdom led her to World Vision, where a collective grant placed over one hundred homeless families into housing through Project Home Again.

In addition to helping the homeless and abused, Mary Nella and her church worked with the gang population. With a goal of getting these kids out of gangs and keeping them off the streets and out of trouble, they opened a youth facility in the open plains of South Dakota. Mary Nella and David sent South Side Chicago's troubled youth there, far from gangs and abject poverty. All but one youth who was relocated to the facility finished school, and many attended Bible college and went on to become productive members of a church and society. And after a short-lived crime spree, the one young exception did eventually go on to become a responsible citizen.

In the midst of pastoring and obtaining grants, a family tragedy occurred. Mary Nella's sister-in-law was diagnosed with terminal cancer. Shortly after diagnosis, she died, leaving two small children, both under three, without a parent. Mary Nella came to the rescue. She and David would adopt the two children and blend them into their existing family of four children, including a new baby. They now had three toddlers and one infant, while still in seminary and pastoring two churches along with accomplishing their community outreach and activism.

As their family grew, so too did the burdens of raising a family in the middle of the dangerous, gang-infested neighborhood they called home. It was time to move to protect their children from the violence. Unable to afford a large-enough home in or around Chicago's better neighborhoods, they left Illinois for Indiana, resulting in an hour's drive to continue their work and ministry. Mary Nella was now forty-three and pregnant with their seventh child. But her energy level was high and her commitment to do God's work unbridled, as she demonstrated after their move.

Not content to sit idly by when a worthy cause needed her help, Mary Nella, as if she had nothing else to do, was stirred to action. It was 1991, and a significant and dreadful problem surfaced in the media: Somalia. It was on the United Nations' radar as a country in trouble and a home to people in great need. The United Nations was sending aid to the war-torn, famine-stricken region in the form of support staff, food, and medical supplies. Nursing her own infant while watching dying babies on the news, Mary Nella prayed and asked God to use her, and this passion to make a difference set her in motion. She subsequently spent one year raising awareness through her newsletter and traveling to Washington, D.C., to meet with lawmakers and Somali immigrants. As a result of her pleas for help, Mary Nella was able to found another nonprofit group, Women Changing the World. Its mission was to work with indigenous women's groups to make changes for the better.

After five trips to Somalia and Kenya, Mary Nella, along with less than a handful of other women, started a relief organization, taught Somalian women how to start and run businesses, and built an orphanage for the children left parentless by death from famine and civil strife. Women Changing the World also founded an orphanage for Nairobi street children in partnership with a local Christian women's organization. When you ask Mary Nella how she liked working in a war-torn country, seeing starvation and rampant disease and senseless maiming and death every day, she responds simply that she loved everything she did in Africa. She needed to be there and they needed her. Those extraordinary women rising from the ashes of their life inspired Mary Nella to be a better person.

Following Mary Nella's courageous work in Africa, her husband decided to lead them back to California to co-pastor a church and raise their children in the Central Valley. Mary Nella reluctantly followed, knowing she'd miss her work in Chicago. Their church experience in

California was wonderful. However, there was never enough money with which to raise their large family. They seemed to be under an ever-increasing and inexplicable mountain of debt. Mary Nella began looking for other work just about the time that David's unrevealed life began to surface.

Arriving back in California, it became glaringly apparent that there was something terribly wrong with her marriage. David's secrecies were growing worse and worse each day. Mary Nella finally discovered the unimaginable. David had an unjustifiable and secret addiction: pornography. Mary Nella realized that her husband of twenty years had been, and continued to be, a habitual liar. In retrospect, Mary Nella readily admits today that much of her church activism was a subtle form of running away; she was focusing on aiding the less fortunate in part so that she wouldn't have to deal with reality at home.

But reality was dealing with her. She could no longer avoid the debt. The house was falling down, literally. The porch fell off the house when one of the girls touched it with her finger, ironically identifying a spot that was likely to give out soon. The banker, when asked by Mary Nella for a loan to repair the porch, suggested that she get out of denial and start dealing with the real world. They were much too far into debt for a loan. Shocked and in disbelief, she asked the banker for proof. He pulled out the documented evidence of unbelievably unmanaged and overextended credit-card debt. Her husband had been squandering money they didn't have, maxing out credit cards to feed his pornography addiction. How, she wondered, could she ever pay it all off on a preacher's salary, or two salaries for that matter?

She left the bank feeling about as low as she could. David continued to refuse to get help or to change his behavior. With college age children, she needed to get their financial house in order to help the children with their education. Her first priority was to stop the financial bleeding by extricating herself from her lying, irresponsible husband. The only option to protect her financial future for the children was to file for divorce. When David heard of her intent, he was livid and adamant that he'd not have any part of it—he would not grant a divorce. Mary Nella turned a deaf ear to his rantings and filed anyway. And the games began. He focused his attention and energy on manipulating the kids, trying with little success to turn them against their mother. Mary Nella kept her focus on the divorce and earning a respectable living. She went job hunting and, much to her delight, landed a decent-paying position as a hospital chaplain for the acutely ill. Her new income would get her and her children by.

But bad went to unimaginably worse. Mary Nella, soon after announcing her intentions of divorce, uncovered a mother's nightmare: the man she had married, the father of her children, had had inappropriate relations with one of their adopted girls. As his deeds unfolded into the light of day, David's behavior became even more bizarre and terrifying. He was breaking down, emotionally and mentally, right before her eyes. Whether his emotions were genuine or manufactured to gain sympathy, they didn't work in either case. She insisted he get help. He refused. Mary Nella wasn't turning back. David finally gave up his fight and signed the divorce papers, promptly leaving town. Mary Nella retained sole custody and legal guardianship of their children, both biological and adopted.

With the divorce behind her, the only looming issue was money. It was still tight, and since her husband was unable and unwilling, she still had to be the one to pay off the debt. Mary Nella couldn't provide for her kids and pay off the debt on one salary alone. Now into her fifties, she accepted the fact that she'd have to take on more work to pay the bills. She added more hospitals to her chaplain work. She also started pastoring in a small church – a three hour commute. She soon found it took all her income to provide the basics: food on the table, a roof over her now-teenage kids' heads, and payment of debts. The time she hoped to have at home with her children was soon lost.

Many nights—after working all day, commuting between hospitals, ministering to the critically ill, comforting the bereaved, and driving the 200-mile loop—she'd be dangerously fatigued behind the wheel of a car. No longer able to see the road, Mary Nella would often pull into truck stops for a few hours of sleep. Then it was time to drive home to get the kids off to school…and do it all over again the next day. Keeping this pace up was an Olympian event, and living in a constant state of exhaustion finally took its toll. Mary Nella found herself with not only a falling-down house, but also a physically, mentally, and emotionally battered body. She could no longer function and had no one to turn to for help but God.

Mary Nella had spent her ministry life praying for others and asking the Lord to meet their needs. Now, in a desperate situation herself, it finally occurred to her to start praying for herself. She often prayed to just have the capacity to get out of bed the next day. Then one day, deep in prayer, the words "love thy neighbor as thyself" echoed in her thoughts. Odd, she thought. She'd spent a lifetime loving her neighbors next door and across continents. There were no boundaries on the love she showered upon strangers and her children. But love thyself? She'd never thought about it until that moment. She realized she needed to find a way to "love herself".

God was answering her prayer. In His way, He reminded Mary Nella that if she weren't able to help herself, she couldn't possibly help others. This one Commandment would change Mary Nella's life. But before it did, she had work to do; she had to discover whom it was that she'd love and try to help. Who was Mary Nella before she was distracted with everyone else? Who had she become after years of living life for others? What did she want and need? No one had ever asked, including herself. Until that moment, Mary Nella had spent much of her adult life submerged in despair and suffering—her own included. In these moments of reflection, Mary Nella realized that what she needed more than anything was a life with far more joy and happiness. It was up to her to make a change.

What she needed immediately was time for introspection. She took a day trip to the desert; alone on a mountain top, surrounded only by the abundance in nature, she saw God's handiwork as far as the eye could see. The quiet around her afforded contemplation. Her prayer was for God to allow her to see herself as she really was, to let go of what others (and herself) had perceived her to be prior to that moment in time. She was in search of the pure, true Mary Nella.

As the desert receded in her rearview mirror four hours later, so did the woman she had arrived as. No more running away from her problems, no more days filled with poverty and deprivation, and no more preaching to others about loving thy neighbor as thyself until she lived what she preached. Instead of praying to God to help her survive the craziness in her old life, she now began praying for guidance and direction for a new life.

"Ask and ye shall receive," the Bible says. As often happens, what you receive is not necessarily what you anticipate it to be. Visiting again with Mary Nella one day, her cousin mentioned that she had started up her network marketing, or multi-level marketing, business again. Having taken a hiatus from it, she had reexamined her life and decided she was going to pour a new energy into her business. She further encouraged Mary Nella to consider signing up. It would be a way to make money and have some fun doing it, she promised. Having no interest in selling products or recruiting others to do so, Mary Nella thanked her cousin but declined the invitation to participate. There had to be another way for a female ordained-minister in her mid-fifties to make a living, she thought.

Desperate for money and time, Mary Nella searched for a new job with no luck. She decided to reconsider her options. She could continue doing what she was doing and experience ever-increasing mental breakdowns, or she could take a look at the business plan her cousin had handed her. She decided to read through it thoroughly. By the time she had finished, Mary Nella was excited. She didn't like selling and cringed at the thought of doing product demonstrations. She did, however, really like the business aspect of helping other people achieve their goals. She would be able to help motivated and happy people build a better life. And the great part was it wouldn't take a lot of money or business knowledge to get started. Mary Nella began to rethink her "no thank you" to her cousin. If this was a way out from the mounds of bills she was drowning under, she'd be crazy not to take it. She decided to give it a shot and learn how to establish her own network marketing business.

Today, Mary Nella is one of the many successful network marketers. She's no longer struggling with debt. She no longer visits her banker looking for loans. She's also defied the naysayers. She's a single woman, close to sixty years old, and for the first time in her life—after only two years at her new job— is well on her way to financial security. She has found joy and happiness that was there all along. When opportunity knocked, this time she opened the door.

A life spent helping others in need goes on for Mary Nella. She is not one to shy away from helping strangers, friends, or family, or from discovering a way over, under, through or around a challenge, however big or small. And she'll guide you along the way. After all, that's always been her true passion in life.

❧   ❧   ❧

Author's Observations:

Although Mary Nella is the first to admit that she gave up much to serve others and sometimes made decisions that weren't necessarily the best, she has left behind a legacy that will live on for generations. Navigating adversities, both her own and those of others, has been her life's mission. When she realized that her life had taken her down a road that wasn't giving her happiness and joy, she set herself on a new course, yet never gave up her role of helping others. She is proof that it only takes one visionary person with courage and determination to make a difference. Her courage in all that she has accomplished in her life makes Mary Nella an extraordinary role model.

CHAPTER TEN

MAVIS

MEET MAVIS SUE ARRINGTON. Mavis is a coal miner's daughter from the mountains of rural western Virginia. Being a miner's child meant either getting married or, more commonly, leaving town after high school graduation. The spoken expectation was that upon graduation, miners' kids headed for college or simply migrated to lands of opportunity—any city would do, as long as it didn't guarantee a life immersed in the mines. Adapting to the rural poverty practically ensured in a mining town was not a life parents wished for their children. Nor was the daily risk to their lives, although miners and their families accepted that danger as a part of the job. Death, either by the Black Lung disease or by mining accidents, was no stranger to those living and working in mining communities, young and old alike. So as expected, and with the encouragement of her parents, Mavis followed the exodus. She, too, left the grit and grime of coal. Unfortunately, Mavis would discover that, try as she might, she couldn't outrun the challenges of extreme adversity that life had in store for her.

Life as a miner's daughter and the youngest child of four (two boys and two girls) was difficult at best. Between school and chores, there was little time for much else but sleep. Survival required that no hands remained idle. There were gardens to tend, laundry to wash, meals to prepare, a house to clean, and food to can for the winter. For Mavis—black-headed as the coal her father mined, brown-eyed, and petite with a shy yet determined personality—being a "good girl" wasn't an option, it was an imperative. The family's reputation and level of respect was of paramount importance in this small community. Tarnishing the family name was not forgotten or undone. Benchmarks for success were not a family's material possessions, but rather how honorably its members behaved. That being said, everyone knew that boys would be boys. But girls were held to an even higher standard.

"Good," for Mavis, was defined by a list of dos and don'ts. Do help with chores, do as you're told, do learn to cope with hardship, and do your schoolwork. Don't date, don't wear makeup, don't cuss, don't wear shorts, don't be disrespectful, don't hang out with boys, don't complain, don't work on Sunday (except for chores), and don't lie or be dishonest. Girls were held to a higher standard in everything. The mines could take their father any day, and wives and children had to be prepared. And after all, it was believed that girls would grow up to become the bedrock of their future families and would need to know how to perform all the duties that would be expected of them: raise children, cook, clean, mend, be a dutiful wife, be frugal, and cope and survive even in the worst of conditions.

Women played an integral role in making life work effectively. Wives and daughters managed survival with modest and oftentimes barely sufficient means. And without them, community support and family did not exist, which were the very things that gave the men purpose for working the mines. Few women ever wallowed in self-pity and if they did, they kept it to themselves. Mavis's young life was spent demonstrating to her mother that she was good. She did as she was told to the best of her abilities. Her mother's standards were high, and the consequences were severe if Mavis disobeyed. She knew at an early age that she would not be the one to bring disgrace upon the family or disappoint her parents. It was the last thing she wanted to do.

Her mother is remembered as a very sad, angry, and more often than not distant and cold woman with metered bouts of kindness. She needed no provocation to unleash her wrath. Her unhappiness may well be attributed to having had dreams of a life beyond the mines. Perhaps it was missed opportunities or the choices she made that caused her to live a life of quiet desperation. If she believed that life had dealt her a bad hand, she made it known to her family through emotions, not words. Outside the confines of home, one would never know the anger she harbored. She presented herself to the community as a loving wife and mother, content with her lot in life and her brood of four children. But at home, she was at times altogether terrifying. It was fear of her mother that imprisoned Mavis into a childhood of silence, obedience, and invisibility.

Her father, on the other hand, was a God-fearing, hardworking, tolerant, and gentle man. He endured his wife's outbursts and remained a loyal husband, father, and provider. For thirty years, during the fall and winter months, he went to work before sunrise, toiled in the mines all day, and returned home after dark, without complaint. He did what he had to and risked his life every day to provide for his family in the only way he knew how. When he wasn't working the mines, he was working the land to feed the livestock and, consequently, his family.

For Mavis, her father was a beacon. It was he who showed her kindness and affection. His gentle spirit and warm smile assured her that she was loved and accepted. It was her father who introduced Mavis to the wonders of the universe; from the song of a bird to the stars in the galaxy, nature was a beauty to behold and a value above and beyond any material possession. Unbeknownst to Mavis in childhood, this soft-spoken, loving man would become her guide as she navigated her way through the many adversities yet to come in her life.

After graduating from high school, Mavis left town, just as her parents expected her to. With her diploma in hand and just four months into her sixteenth year, she boarded a bus for the bright lights of Washington, D.C., and secured a clerical job with the FBI. She not only had to learn her new job, but she also had to acquire the social and people skills necessary to function adequately in the big city. As a country girl from a mining town, she had been taught highly useful self-sufficiency skills, but she quickly discovered that city life demanded an entirely different set of survival skills.

Mavis arrived in Washington, D.C., feeling like she had arrived in a foreign land. Nothing was familiar; no part of the city culture or its people reminded her of home. But "home" was no longer the rural southwest Virginia mountains. It was where Mavis now lived: a boarding house in the heart of the city. One day, a co-worker invited Mavis to share her one-bedroom apartment. She jumped at the chance, thinking it would be the perfect arrangement. Instead, Mavis discovered too late that her new roommate was a party animal. She and her friends entertained the Marines from the nearby base every night and went to work exhausted the following day. While Mavis moved in thinking that nighttime was for sleeping, she quickly learned that nighttime could also be for partying, drinking, and meeting boys. She had no choice but to join in until her finances improved. But before she could afford to move out, Mavis met, and shortly afterward married, one of the late-night-partying Marines. He, she believed, was different from the others. He was thoughtful and kind and didn't ignore her as the others did. It was a kindness she had been thirsting for since she had left her father.

Married and now in Baltimore with her new husband, their first and only child arrived sooner than expected. They were now the proud parents of a baby boy, David. Their military salary, however, came to an end. Her husband left the Marines in pursuit of a career as a musician. Life was about to become overwhelming for Mavis. With a sporadically-employed husband and a new baby, there was no financial stability. She managed to persevere for her son's sake by her grit and her solid work ethic, learned in childhood. But it wasn't easy, by any means. Out of work most of the time, her husband began to exhibit unsavory characteristics: drinking, partying, seeing other women, and—most devastatingly—physically abusing his wife. Barely an adult herself, Mavis soon realized she had two children on her hands: her young son and her husband. Living with a man who was abusive, shunned responsibility, and behaved like an out-of-control teenager was intolerable. Removing her son from an unhealthy and destructive environment became her obsession.

When a friend offered her home to Mavis and David, she jumped at the chance to move out and raise her son free from physical abuse and emotional torment. But after a few years of single motherhood and a growing son, Mavis made a decision that was met with intense disdain from her mother. She met and married Shiivaram, a man from India. He was alone and outcast, as was Mavis as a divorcée with a child. It was a marriage of mutual convenience, but sadly was not accepted by either of their families. He was outcast from his family for marrying her, and she was not allowed home for marrying him. The marriage lasted a year. Divorced again and old enough to recognize the discrimination against single mothers even within her own family, Mavis had to make a change for the better.

At twenty-six, Mavis decided that she and David should move back to her roots in western Virginia. It would be easier to raise a child as a single mother near a support system than continue to go it alone in a big city. However, two strikes were immediately against Mavis upon her return: two failed marriages and single parenthood. In her hometown, "good' girls didn't do either. Her mother, she knew, would become a constant reminder of her transgressions and the shame she had brought home with her. With her father, though, she knew that his love, acceptance, and emotional support would be unconditional. It didn't matter that Mavis had failed at marriage twice, nor did it matter that she was the first family member to divorce. He was delighted that Mavis had brought a grandson into the world, and the fact that she'd returned home with his grandson was a source of pride for him until his death many years later.

The value that she found in motherhood and within her father's love was the glue that kept Mavis together and allowed her to function even with the baggage her mother kept loading onto her back. Although her mother's attacks on her character were hurtful, Mavis reminded herself that her mission was not to please her mother or to remove the shame on her family, but to raise her son to the best of her ability. If she kept focused on the important things and did not become distracted by her mother's emotional dysfunctions, she'd achieve her goal.

Shortly after her arrival back in Virginia, she met Gerald. There were not many eligible bachelors in rural Virginia, and certainly not many willing to seriously date a divorced woman with a child. His availability and interest in Mavis was a godsend to her parents. They encouraged the relationship and hoped that they'd marry—Gerald would bring some respectability to Mavis. He was kind, considerate, outgoing, and accepting of Mavis and David…so much so that David often accompanied them on their dates. Eighteen months later, they married, very much in love.

But soon after the honeymoon period ended, Mavis discovered Gerald had a plan. He decided she needed "fixing." She became his project, as he convinced her to talk, act, and dress perfectly, in his eyes. Determined not to cause trouble, to be the dutiful wife and stay married this time, Mavis did as she was told and changed as she was instructed to. She also became pregnant with Douglas, their son and David's stepbrother. With Gerald's acceptance of David as his own and the respectability their marriage had renewed for her family, Mavis kept her feelings of regret buried deep within. She didn't like being judged at every turn, but failing at this marriage was out of the question. She'd endure whatever was necessary to make it work.

The boys grew, and the marriage held tenuously together. Mavis didn't change much on the inside, but on the outside she cloaked herself in the changes Gerald tried to instill in her, for appearance's sake as well as to keep the peace at home. As the months turned into years, Mavis began to understand that Gerald, like so many self-appointed fixers, never finished his projects. So as their years together progressed, Mavis figured out the hurtful realization that she'd never be "perfect" enough for Gerald. Regardless of how hard she tried and how much she had changed, something about her would always require more improvement.

In the midst of her emotional distress with her husband, Mavis experienced the incomparably painful process of losing her father to cancer, watching life make its slow departure from his fragile body. When her own developing health problems began to materialize, including several cancer scares, Mavis made a decision. Life was too short and too unpredictable to spend it trying to be somebody she wasn't. She needed to find herself and discover who she was at her core. Mavis was going to fix Mavis.

While she continued to focus her attention on her two boys, she also began to reveal her true thoughts and opinions, likes and dislikes, and wants and needs. Slowly, Mavis introduced her real self to Gerald and her sons. Gerald was taken aback with his new wife. He worked overtime trying to regain his power over her, while Mavis worked overtime struggling to hang on to her newly assertive self. The boys, she decided, were going to be her top priority. She would do whatever it took to give them the opportunity to go to college and obtain degrees—to have the chance to make something of themselves and not settle for the crumbs in life. Whatever happened between she and Gerald would not interfere with her sons' future if she could help it.

As Mavis became more independent and resisted Gerald's manipulations, the tension between them grew. But after time, they found that their differences were numerous but manageable. Love was still somewhere in the mix; their commonalities were enough to sustain their marriage. And Mavis's health problems contributed to an unspoken agreement between them to weather the storms together. It was less than ideal, but it was what it was, and Mavis, like so many others, would make the best of it.

By her early forties, Mavis suffered her first of a series of strokes. Prior to reaching her fiftieth birthday, she suffered her first heart attack and learned she had adult onset diabetes, Lupus immunity disorder, a shut-down kidney, and severe arthritis in her neck caused by a car accident many years earlier, limiting the mobility of her hands and arms. Since these diagnoses, the past ten years have dealt Mavis even more health blows. On oxygen and unable to walk or exert herself for longer than five to ten minutes, she now travels by a four-wheeled scooter, equipped with an oxygen tank holder. Most recently, Mavis was diagnosed with Parkinson's disease after suffering bouts of uncontrollable shaking.

With her deteriorating health and limited mobility, Mavis realized her thirty-year marriage to a man she loved had now become one of necessity. Yet when she honestly assessed her marriage, she realized that Gerald was rarely there for her. He was unable to cope with Mavis's increasing ailments and dependence upon him. He spent his days far from home and unavailable to Mavis. If Mavis had an urgent need or a doctor's appointment, he managed to get home in time to drive her. Otherwise, Mavis lived alone. As the months passed, Mavis couldn't help but contemplate making a change. Their wedding vows were specific: they would love and cherish one another "in sickness and in health." For Gerald, it seemed emotionally impossible for him to care for his wife in failing health. The knowledge that her husband was unwilling to be there for her in her time of need caused Mavis extreme emotional pain on top of her physical problems. It was devastating to feel his rejection day after day, month after month. She couldn't change her failing health; that was out of her hands. But she still had the power to make a change in her marriage.

In May of 2006, Mavis made the most difficult decision of her life. Gerald couldn't cope with Mavis and her condition, and Mavis couldn't cope with Gerald's avoidance and escape. She made up her mind to file for divorce and stop the pain of rejection and abandonment. She would pour her energy into handling her life-threatening health conditions and her family. But how would she manage on her own? she asked herself countless times. The answer was always the same: just like she had been doing all along while married to an absentee husband. She also can count on David and Douglas. At thirty-nine and twenty-eight years of age respectively, they have wisdom beyond their years and a love for their mother that had no conditions and no boundaries. She won't have to go through this difficult time alone.

Today, Mavis has decided to leave the Virginian home she's known since childhood. Her eldest son, David, has his doctorate in pharmacology and lives in Knoxville, Tennessee. He has convinced Mavis to move into an assisted-living facility close to him, so he can look after her medications and her care. Douglas has become the family attorney as well as the assistant district attorney for the county in which he was born and raised. He will look after and live on the family homestead. Douglas's presence will offer comfort and peace for Mavis when she visits, as will wrapping her frail arms around her youngest joy, her five-year-old grandson Dylan.

Mavis's declining health and her dependence on outside assistance continue to increase as time goes on. But ask her about her quality of life and she'll tell you it's pretty darn good. Her sons, daughters-in-law, and little Dylan are the forces that sustain her positive attitude and give meaning to her life. She also embraces the things most of us take for granted: our families, friends, and the abundance of joy derived from the gift of nature, a love passed along from her father. It's not been easy—divorce never is. And when you compound divorce with fragile health and a move far from home, it can be overwhelming. But with courage in the face of adversity and much love from family and friends, Mavis will live on knowing she has been blessed.

🌿 🌿 🌿

Author's Observations:

Inner strength and a dedication to letting her individuality shine through have been the pillars throughout Mavis's challenging life. Despite her acute physical disabilities, Mavis spent her time and energy focusing on what she could do, rather than what she couldn't. Her independence and high sense of self-worth made her confident that she could survive her extremely difficult circumstances without her husband's feigned support. She navigated her way through some hurtful and devastating choices with determination and courage, choosing to surround herself with the love of her devoted family. As some doors closed, Mavis discovered that others had opened—and she walked through them.

CHAPTER ELEVEN

CHRISTIE

MEET CHRISTIE SHOWS. If you've ever thought that teenage drinking was harmless fun, just kids being kids, think again. Christie, like so many other adolescents, was a teenage alcoholic. Although no one knew it at the time, Christie was well on her way to becoming an out-of-control addict. Alcohol was her gateway to pot in her teens; pot was her entrée into snorting cocaine in her twenties and when that wasn't enough, she turned to the granddaddy of all speeds, methamphetamine, before reaching the age of thirty. Then one day her alcohol and drug addiction abruptly stopped—but not by choice.

Christie was born and spent her early childhood in Montgomery, Alabama. After her parents divorced, her mother remarried. Her new stepfather was in the United States Air Force, shattering any chance of stability in Christie's life. As a military family, Christie and her three brothers moved seven times before graduating high school. For Christie, partying and drinking was the fastest way to fit in and quickly establish new friends. It took only a few moves to figure out that if she didn't make acquaintances fast, she would have no friends before the next move. With no family roots or community ties, she had no reason to worry about her reputation; she never stuck around anywhere long enough for it to matter.

By the end of high school, even the loss of her biological father due to alcohol abuse did nothing to deter Christie from drinking. If anything, it gave her cause to ramp it up to a higher, more intense level. Her parents' divorce, a merry-go-round of making new friends, and her father's death caused her to stuff her emotions deep inside her and rely on her addictions for insentience. Life was a nonstop party; slowing down might have meant having to deal with the emotional pain that was feeding her insecurities and resentments. By eighteen years of age, Christie was numbing herself into a life of separation and loss.

Standing apart from her well-adjusted brothers, Christie became known as the family's black sheep. While her brothers embraced their learned values and acted according to their moral compasses for right and wrong, Christie took on the attitude of "if it feels good, do it." Drinking and drugs felt good, so she did both. Eventually, sick and tired of her reckless and abusive behavior, her brothers disowned her and her stepfather distanced himself from her life. She was a hopeless case, completely uncontrollable, too wild and crazy; her family—even her amazingly supportive mother—was convinced there was little hope for her.

After high school, Christie drifted, finally ending up in New Orleans. It was the perfect environment for her. Lots of drinking and good times rolled day and night in New Orleans. Contrary to many addicts, Christie was never adverse to work. She had been taught a strong work ethic, and apparently there was enough glue in the teachings to have it stick. She worked as a bartender, did odd jobs like painting, and worked in sales. She did whatever it took to feed her addictions and keep a roof over her head. By the time she reached New Orleans, marijuana was merely kid's play. After all, she'd graduated from high school—she was an adult. So she turned to the harder stuff and began snorting cocaine. And with this change, feeding her habit became more costly. Odd jobs wouldn't cover it. She needed to make more money.

Having had some success in sales, Christie turned to selling drugs. It was the logical choice for her. With her family back in

California, she had nobody watching or judging her. What she didn't tell them, they wouldn't know. In no time, with her personality and her demeanor signifying that she had been raised well, Christie realized she had what it took to be an uptown drug dealer. She could sell drugs to the professionals: the judges, lawyers, doctors, executives, police, and politicians. They could trust that she was "one of them." She didn't have the professional credentials, but she did know how to act in their presence and among their colleagues and friends. Her clientele was sophisticated and upscale. Because of this, she was known as a sophisticated and upscale dealer and with that recognition, she could justify feeling good about herself. She lost her moral compass but justified her actions by her associations with the city's "most respected." She was somebody meaningful within the social circles of the powerful. Her position also offered her protection from prosecution. In short, she seemed to have it made.

In the early 1980s when Nancy Reagan, our nation's First Lady, began her "Just Say No to Drugs" campaign, life changed for Christie. "It pissed me off," Christie says with a smile. With her booming drug business and her respectable reputation as a high-end dealer, "Just Say No" sharply impacted her sales. Some of her clients reduced their frequency of use, while others quit altogether. Dealers who were once given a pass by the police were now being arrested. Her supply chain was cut off abruptly. As sales dwindled, her income plummeted. With her uptown clientele dried up, Christie was forced to find new customers. These users would not be in the same class as those she had become accustomed to dealing with. These customers lived in the seedier and more dangerous part of town. She had a decision to make: suck it up and work the low-end drug market of addicts or find a new line of work. But a new career would also mean kicking the drug habit, which she wasn't of a mind to do.

During this time, Christie abandoned drinking after a fellow bartender caught her trying to pocket his tips. Her attempted tip theft was a sobering moment for her. It was really the first time over the course of ten years that she had ever stopped to think about what she was doing and who she'd become. She recalls the alarm she felt when she realized she had sunk to the level of petty thievery. She was certain that it was alcohol, not drugs, that had caused her moral failure. So although she quit drinking, she ramped up her drug habit. This ethically bereft experience marked the beginning of Christie's downfall.

Christie had by now completely lost any sense of moral direction her parents had instilled in her. She had rationalized and justified her choice as a career drug dealer. Her upscale clientele had made it so easy, since she was respected and accepted into an elite social environment; odd jobs didn't provide this kind of respectability or importance. She also believed, in her drug-induced state, that these people were her friends. She was clueless that her only value to them was as a dealer. They had no other commonalities. Their rejection of her when the "Just Say No" campaign hit was something she had never anticipated. But Christie decided that even though she'd lost her more lucrative and upscale "friends" as clients, she would continue selling drugs anyway. The seedier part of town proved to be more than just seedy, though. It was also far more competitive than the upscale market, and consequently making money became much more difficult. Blinded by her desperation to earn a living and by being a user herself, she became reckless. In a matter of months, she found herself in handcuffs, arrested and facing felony charges for drug dealing.

Now a convicted criminal at age thirty-three, sitting in jail awaiting her sentencing, Christie decided to clean up her act. She hadn't been raised to do this. If her family found out, they'd be appalled. So she vowed to stop selling and using drugs. She also decided to move back to California, leaving New Orleans and all she'd become behind her. It would be a fresh start among her family, who had no idea what she had really been doing in New Orleans. After her release on probation, she moved back to California, got a job, and worked for several years, remaining clean and sober. She even attained her real estate appraiser's license. But temptation was like a shadow, constantly stepping on her heels. While appraising properties, she discovered that drugs were plentiful around construction sites. One fateful day, her willpower collapsed. After six years of being drug- and alcohol-free and living by the morals and values she was raised with, Christie caved to temptation. It would become the worst decision of her life.

One day, after working her way back into the drug scene, there was a dispute between Christie and another woman while Christie was high on meth. The other woman's side of the argument escalated to threats of inflicting harm against Christie and her family. Not taking kindly to the threats, Christie left immediately, swearing that she would return and show this woman that threats bring consequences. That night, she poured gasoline around the perimeter of the woman's garage, tossed a lit match, and burned it to the ground. Everything in it turned to ash, including the woman's mother's antiques and a lifetime of her mother's family mementos.

Enraged, the woman told the arson investigators that she was certain who did it and why. After tracking Christie down and giving little credence to her alibi, investigators found sufficient evidence to charge her with arson and another felony drug charge. But this was not going to be like New Orleans. She was not going to be released on probation without serving any time. This time, in her drug-induced condition, she had crossed the line. Arson was a felony of huge magnitude by law enforcement standards. Although denying her involvement in the arson in order to protect her family from abject humiliation and an overwhelming sense of failure and shame, Christie was found guilty and sentenced to five years in prison. It was 1995, and she was just three days shy of turning forty. Instead of planning a party for this milestone birthday, she was surrounded by armed guards on her way to the Chowchilla Valley State Prison for Women.

Thoughts of how deeply wounded her family would be by her actions, as well as how deeply she had wounded herself, played nonstop en route to the prison. Her mother, believing her daughter to be innocent, stuck by the story Christie had told her. It was unfathomable to her that her daughter could have committed such a crime. With her belief so solid in Christie's innocence, she became Christie's rock. Although Christie knew it was based on a lie, her mother's belief in her gave her the impetus to want to start over when she got out of prison. Her stepfather, on the other hand, kept his distance from her. And her three brothers would not even admit that Christie was their sibling.

Filled with guilt about her lies to her mother, deep shame from her corrupt actions, and unimaginable sadness from losing her loved ones, Christie was as low as she could get. But she had more than just her own ugly emotions to deal with now. Prison is not a model environment. If you don't know the ugly side of human nature before you enter, you'll learn it before you get out. Prison, first and foremost, is about survival. And being tough and street-smart are the prerequisites—the faint of heart won't make it. Christie had learned many survival skills when dealing drugs, but nothing had prepared her for what she'd find on a cell block. She learned very fast that before she could fix herself and her character flaws, she'd first have to figure out how to stay safe. She was surrounded by delusional and terrifying women. Inmates would torment her if they spotted her vulnerabilities. She had to learn how to live like an inmate and how to defend and protect herself every minute of every day. "I learned what 'really bad' meant in there," she reflects.

Prison life for Christie was going to be one of two options: working—in her case, in the Prison Industry Authority (PIA)—or sitting on the cell block all day commiserating with other inmates. Christie chose the PIA route, hoping for a chance to learn some skills she could use upon her release from prison. It would keep her busy doing something productive, and maybe she could find a few women like herself, those looking to clean up their acts and become meaningful contributors to society. But as Christie spoke of her wish to make something of herself, the naysayers told her over and over that convicted felons can't make their way in society because no one will hire them. The desire to learn new skills, the commitment she made to herself to never relive her past, and her dream to succeed through the opportunities provided by the PIA were met with mocking laughter. How stupid could she be to believe that anyone would be convinced she was rehabilitated—that she could or would return to society a responsible citizen? Christie kept telling herself they were wrong, and that she'd prove it when she got out.

Having secured a job in the PIA's optical department, Christie began learning how to make lenses for eyeglasses. Her glasses and safety wear were supplied to inmates around the state, other state agencies, Medi-Cal, and nonprofit organizations. There was plenty of work to keep Christie and her fellow inmates busy five days a week, year in and year out. In time, Christie kept her commitment to herself and became one of the most knowledgeable and skilled technicians the PIA had. At forty-three, Christie clearly recognized that she had done nothing of any real value since she started drinking and smoking pot in high school. And as an adult, she had not had any successes without the aid of drugs or alcohol, other than a few years when she was clean upon her return to California. But what she was doing now in the PIA's optical division gave her a lasting, drug-free high for the first time in her life.

With a five-year sentence for arson, Christie was advised that she'd be released two years early due to good behavior. With this news came a whole new set of challenges. First, where would she live? Her stepfather really didn't want her to live with him and her mother. But her mother—her only visitor during her incarceration—wanted to give her a chance. Her stepfather finally reluctantly agreed to a temporary living arrangement with Christie with strict conditions, none of which were a problem for Christie. Whatever his rules, she'd abide by each one of them without exception.

Finally, in 1998, after three long years, Christie walked through the clanging steel prison gates to her freedom. Even though she was on parole, she could sleep nights without the incessant loud noise of other inmates, eat what she wanted to eat, and come and go without guard escorts. Now she needed to find a job. Work would require some decent work clothes and transportation. It would also require a shift in her attitude about the world around her. She had to shed the vocabulary of prison and be mindful of what she said and how she said it; she needed to cast off the survival mode she was taught in prison.

Her fellow inmates' warnings of a lack of good jobs for convicted felons were not far from her mind. She vowed to not let their pessimistic attitudes sink her into their defeatist trap. If she dared to believe them, she knew she would be back in prison within the year. She pledged to do work no one else wanted to do, just to prove to her employer she was determined to make good. She refused to believe there was no life after prison; there had to be. Settling for nothing would not be an option. She opened her mother's telephone book and found the numbers for the three big optical chains in the area. She called each one in search of employment. To her surprise, she was invited in for an interview by all three.

With the money she'd earned at the PIA, Christie bought some work-worthy clothes, feeling certain one of the optical companies would hire her to do something, even if she had to start as a janitor. Then she rummaged through her stepfather's stored belongings from his working years and found an old, worn briefcase. She dusted it off, shined it up, and carried it with her to her interviews. She would look professional if nothing else, even though all she had in it were résumés. She didn't have enough money for a car, so she used the public county bus for her transportation. It took longer to get where she needed to go, but she scheduled her interviews far enough apart to avoid being late. Any one of these interviews, if successful in gaining employment, would require a minimum one-hour commute each way. But it didn't matter. The job was what mattered to her. Whatever she had to do, she was committed to doing it.

Her mind-set entering each meeting was focused on getting a job to prove to herself and everyone else that she could and would be a productive member of society. She also wanted to prove to her fellow inmates that they were wrong. Felons can change, and she'd set the example. During each interview, Christie readily admitted she was a convicted felon and that she had committed the crimes of arson and drug possession. But she also told them of her incarceration and her success in the optical division of the PIA. In addition, she made an offer to each prospective employer. She volunteered to take on a job nobody else wanted. She told them she'd come in early and leave late. She said she'd do all that was required of her and more, if there was work to be done and if she had the skills to do it. And she closed each interview by promising them that she would not just meet their expectations, she would exceed them. All she asked for was a chance.

In the days that followed, Christie received job offers not just from one, but from all three employers. She was overjoyed, euphoric in her new life without any artificial stimulation. She had accomplished what only her PIA optical supervisor had believed that she could. It didn't matter that she'd start at the bottom and work her way up. She knew if she got in the door, she'd prove herself, and promotions would follow. And that's exactly what happened. She was hired as a part-time gofer and given a chance to show management what she could do. Before the end of her first year, Christie had become the general manager of the LensCrafters flagship store, turning out sales numbers they'd never seen before. She had also enrolled in a community college and attended classes when she wasn't working. Impressed, her superiors saw Christie as a greater asset to the company every passing day. As a result, Christie was sent to other stores as a corporate regional training expert; she showed other managers how to succeed by meeting and exceeding sales goals. Eighteen months after her first day on the job as a gofer, Christie became one of LensCrafters's most valued employees. Its gamble on an ex-con had paid off handsomely.

Christie stayed with LensCrafters for five years before leaving to make a difference within the California Department of Corrections as an inmate employment specialist. She teaches the soft skills and attitudes that had worked so well for her. In addition, Christie has now become an entrepreneur, starting a business venture on the side with a colleague from LensCrafters.

Today, with her family relationships restored, Christie is flourishing. Although her mother passed away from cancer on January 1, 2002, she lived to see Christie recapture and embrace the morals and ethics her mother and stepfather worked so hard to instill in her. She died a proud mother with her daughter by her side, a place

Christie had been for many months during her illness—just like her mother had been at Christie's side during her worst moments. Today, her stepfather is her best friend. The love, earned respect, and pride between them today were unimaginable to both a few short years ago. He is currently in the early to middle stages of Alzheimer's disease, and Christie is his confidante, able to care for him now like he did for her.

Today, drugs and prison have been left in the far past, along with the naysayers. Christie is an accomplished woman, on a mission to prove that no adversity is too difficult to navigate. There are no past behaviors that can't be changed or failed reputations that can't be repaired, if you persevere and stay confident, applying the skills you learn in life along the way.

🌿　🌿　🌿

Author's Observations:

Unlike many other women who face seemingly insurmountable challenges, Christie was in complete control of her own life, with nobody else—such as a husband or a significant other—calling the shots. She had the opportunity to decide which path in life she wanted to go down, and whether she wanted to throw her life away once and for all or pick up the pieces and start over. Once she stopped rationalizing her deviant behavior, she was finally able to look at her life with open eyes. Her shame and humiliation at what she saw motivated her to remake herself into a woman she and her family could be proud of. She ignored the pessimists who said she'd never recover from her past, instead making a conscious decision to defy the odds: to earn respect and achieve success in life. Christie used the same remarkable fortitude and ambition that she'd used to make herself a felon to instead make herself a responsible and successful member of society.

CHAPTER TWELVE

EDIE

MEET EDIE WEST. She's soft-spoken, a quiet observer of her surroundings until it's her turn to speak. That's when you detect the accomplished woman behind her gentle but enthusiastic nature. She's the one who makes every other person feel like the most important person in the room. It's a skill she learned growing up as a preacher's daughter. She is so good at it, in fact, that she has authored the books *201 Icebreakers* and *The Big Book of Icebreakers* in order to share some of her conversational magic with others. But as you can probably surmise by now, Edie's life hasn't been as easy as her outward persona might lead you to believe.

Born and raised in Deptford, New Jersey, Edie was one of four children—a middle child with two sisters and a brother—born to Harry and Harriet Sink. Harry was a non-denominational Christian pastor, best known for his passion for building churches and establishing solid foundations of committed parishioners. Backed by his unshakable faith, he ensured that believers had a place to worship and share their religion, trials, and tribulations. He built and established two churches, staying at his last one for thirty-five years until his death at age seventy-two. Edie had what many would consider a blessed relationship with both her mother and father; she was loved, respected, and valued by both. But although she was close with both parents, Edie forged a bond with Harry in a way that only loving fathers and daughters can.

Edie's mother, Harriet, was a homemaker as well as a preacher's wife. Raising four children combined with supporting a church congregation produced two full-time jobs, in this case held by one woman. Neither children nor congregants checked her schedule before their needs arose. In these dual roles, Harriet learned to adapt and be flexible. Edie, like her siblings, was taught early on that service to God and others was not only honorable, it was also the critical component of character development. "My wants and needs come first" was considered to be an unthinkable and unacceptable attitude. These early teachings would set the stage for Edie's unfailing and lifelong commitment to aiding her parents.

Edie and her brother and sisters grew up without riches or luxuries. Although there was always enough money to satisfy their needs and sometimes even enough for a small family vacation, money was still hard to come by. Building a church from a handful of parishioners left Harry's family with responsibilities that were oftentimes greater than their available resources. Yet they were solid and united in their mission to be of service to others, and their lack of abundant financial resources never deterred Pastor Sink. He worked on the side as a carpenter and an overseer as time permitted, coming home each evening to shower, eat, and continue with the work of the Lord. His conviction was rock solid that if one believed, the Lord would always provide. Harry's faith, teachings, and actions sustained his family and his church through a myriad of crises and heartaches. He was not only adored by his own children, but everyone he knew—children, teens, and adults alike—revered him until the end. He left a legacy of making a difference in the lives of all he touched.

Edie spent her waking hours attending school, doing homework, and participating in church-sponsored events and services. Her love and respect for her family, the community, and their church ran too deep for her to want to bring shame to them in any way. However, Edie did have a spark of independence about her, a trait no doubt passed along from her father. This independence didn't cause her to outwardly rebel, but it did entice her to step outside the boundaries of her family's faith; specifically, these restrictions involved no dancing, no make-up, very limited dating, and no hanging out with kids after school. Edie's social life was intended to be completely focused on the church.

But Edie's quest to discover her own identity and the world beyond the church caused her to circumvent restrictions when opportunities arose—although that wasn't very often. Sundays she spent in Sunday school and then church services; Tuesday evenings she attended various mission outreaches where she played the piano; Wednesdays she went to prayer meetings with more piano playing; Thursdays she spent with the church family at either a potluck or a picnic; Fridays she dedicated to Bible Club; Saturdays she went to Youth for Christ and played yet more piano; and Sundays the whole routine started all over again. What little free time Edie did have to express her independence was spent wearing lipstick at school, dancing at classmates' homes, spending time with her friends (including boys), and naturally omitting the whole truth regarding her whereabouts to her family. Because she, like her parents, disliked smoking and drinking alcohol, her secrets were subtle and therefore easy to keep.

After her high school graduation, Edie was accepted and enrolled at Taylor University, a Christian university in Indiana. However, that experience was short-lived, as Edie became more and more homesick and heartsick for her high school sweetheart. After her freshman year, she left Indiana and enrolled in Eastern Baptist College (now Eastern University) in Pennsylvania, near her New Jersey roots and her beau. After receiving her degree in English, Edie taught school for a year and became engaged to her boyfriend.

Consumed with becoming a bona fide adult, Edie dreamily envisioned her wedding day when her brother Harry Sinex Sink, also a minister, would perform her marriage ceremony. But this was never to be. Harry Sinex Sink suffered from a tragic and crippling disease. On the day before her wedding, he endured a severe attack and had to be hospitalized. The situation should have been expected; he had tried to warn Edie on a couple of occasions. He knew he was going to die sooner rather than later, and he wanted her to be prepared. But Edie, in her naiveté and hopefulness, would not listen. With the substitution of her brother's good friend as the minister, the wedding went on. But what should have been one of the happiest events of her life turned into a bittersweet occasion that she endured through a haze of mixed emotions. Later, when Edie was pregnant with her first child, Harry Sinex Sink—only thirty-four years old—died. She felt the pain of this loss acutely.

Immediately following their wedding, the newlyweds moved to Burlington, Vermont, where her husband entered the University of Vermont while Edie taught school and eventually left teaching for an administrative position. The marriage modeled the wedding, infused simultaneously with both joy and pain. After raising two boys— Ron and Todd—and eighteen years of marriage, their relationship collapsed. Meaningful and constructive communication had become nonexistent. Contrary to all that Edie had been taught growing up, society's influence outside the protected environment of her parents and church had taken hold and slowly eroded the foundation of their once rock-solid marriage. Divorce wasn't considered an acceptable remedy according to Edie's upbringing, but their increasingly selfish and inflexible marriage certainly couldn't go on. The impact of the divorce on her parents was lessened somewhat by her father's death just before the announcement of their separation.

Edie and her husband had moved to Altamont, New York, just a few years before their split. Edie had given up her career in education and said good-bye to her closest friends in order to support her husband in his job relocation. She had started working for the state and eventually began migrating into self-employment as a business consultant, teaching employees fundamental skill sets so they could flourish in the corporate environment. But divorce comes with a price—literally. In Edie's case, she was determined to protect her sons as much as she could and try to maintain their standard of living. She took out a second mortgage on her house, using the money to offset their reduced income and provide a buffer while she established her consulting business. For the boys, life went on as it had before—with sports, extracurricular activities, and soon college educations.

However, Edie soon discovered she wasn't as strong and invincible as she thought she was. About six years after she and her husband went their separate ways, she experienced an emotional setback that was worse than anything she had encountered before. During this time, she not only fought for emotional survival, but also for financial stability. Unable to do as much work during this difficult time, she relied on help from friends and put bills on hold until she could manage them. Edie had always believed that all things happen for a reason—this time was no exception. When she found herself worrying and feeling so helpless, the words she had heard so often from her beloved father began to echo in her mind: "The Lord always provides to those with faith." Edie's past began to play a vital role in her present. Her unshakeable faith, along with her steadfast commitment to her sons and her perseverance in preserving her young business, got her back on course. She discovered that focusing solely on herself didn't create the happiness she'd expected. Her inner rebellion and self-centeredness receded, and her commitment to serving God and others became much more meaningful in her life. Her future began to take shape.

Then, one day, fate stepped in. After spending a few days with her ailing mother, Edie was waiting in the Philadelphia airport for a return flight home when a gentleman named Glenn struck up a conversation with her.. What began as idle dialogue soon evolved into a feeling for each other beyond words. Edie and Glenn quickly discovered that they had much in common. He managed a retirement center and was a kindly and caring soul. His passion for the well-being of the elderly population, his unwavering faith in the Lord, and the occurrence of his recent divorce were topics that Edie could relate to. After all, her own mother, Harriet, was in failing health and it was only a matter of time until she'd need direct oversight—by Edie herself, as it would turn out. Glenn, too, was committed to caring for his father, as his mother had died just two years earlier.

Time did run out, as their flights were departing. But they agreed to reconnect soon. And after five months of weekend dates, Glenn and Edie married. Between them, they had their deep love, their faith, their commitment to care for their parents, and their children —but they had little money. Yet their belief that the Lord would provide gave them peace of mind that they would find a way to dig out of an ever-deepening hole.

Edie moved to Virginia to Glenn's home, just outside of Washington, DC. After they settled in, she continued her consulting business to a lesser degree, dabbled in developing products for trainers, and began writing the book 201 Icebreakers. (This book and her next, The Big Book of Icebreakers, have since become invaluable reference tools for professional and social use.) Still she and Glenn struggled to make ends meet. But soon their prayers were answered. Edie was hired as executive director of a newly created federal commission. Her increased salary allowed her and Glenn to buy a new home that could be built with the modifications necessary to accommodate Edie's mother and Glenn's father. Edie and Glenn remained committed to caring for their parents when it was obvious they could no longer care for themselves. And that time was nearing fast, as their most recent visits indicated.

In 1997, Edie and Glenn were working full time in demanding jobs when Harriet, at eighty- five years of age, moved into their home. The adjustment was not an easy one. Both Edie and her mother had to accept the reversal of the roles they'd each held for nearly fifty years, with Edie now caring for her mother rather than receiving her mother's care herself. Adapting to changing circumstances is always difficult, but more often than not it's made much easier within loving environments. Edie had grown up with the love and wholehearted devotion of her parents, and her mother's inevitable sacrifices made on Edie's behalf over the years made the decision a clear one. Edie knew her home was the place for her mother to live out her remaining days, no matter how difficult and burdensome the situation. "It was the right thing to do," says Edie.

And burdensome it would become. Being uprooted to a new community and a new house after more than sixty years, along with losing her independence, was emotionally and physically unsettling to Harriet. In Edie's case, her life became a juggling act between caring for her children, adjusting to married life again, meeting the demands of a new job, and dealing with her mother during some rough transitional times. As if all that wasn't enough, Edie was also battling fibromyalgia. Symptoms of this frustrating condition include pain in muscles and soft tissue, bouts of extreme fatigue, and restless sleep; there is no known cure. For Edie, it was especially difficult dealing with fibromyalgia during a period of such significant change in her life, but she coped as best as she could. Harriet began to adjust to her new environment and accept the fact she was no longer able to live on her own. She missed her familiar surroundings and her independence, but she recognized her blessing to have a daughter and new son-in-law willingly and lovingly give her their home to spend her final years. Edie imposed no guilt upon her mother for disrupting their lives, instead making it clear that she was acting as she was out of love and a deep sense of honor.

Glenn's father, Walter, came to live with Glenn and Edie about three years after Harriet had moved in. His time in the West household, however, was limited. After just a few short months experiencing an ever-worsening Parkinson's disease, he realized his need for more intensive care and entered the nursing section of the retirement community where Glenn served as executive director. Glenn stopped and spent time with his father each night before coming home, and Edie visited him as well whenever she could.

As the months turned into years, Harriet's care went from mild checkups and doctor's appointments to memory loss and more intense homebound care. Her mother's increasingly failing health began to put an additional burden on Edie. It was becoming harder to leave for work and trust that all was well at home. And with Edie's own health problems more and more problematic as well, something had to change. A nursing home for her mother was out of the question. Edie had made a promise to God and her mother that she would care for her mother herself. Edie's siblings had their own busy lives and were not an option for caregiving. Then a ray of light entered their lives. Edie's oldest son, Ron, and his wife moved into the downstairs apartment of Glenn and Edie's home. Now somebody was always in the house, which was particularly helpful for Glenn and Edie's careers. The newcomers also brought two other members to the household: first a boy and then, three years later, a girl. Now there were four generations under the same roof—a blessed arrangement for Edie's mother, but unfortunately not as easy for the other four adults. Eventually, Ron and his family moved to their own home about twelve miles away.

But once again, God had a plan. As Edie and Glenn prayed about their circumstances, Edie was notified that the commission she had been hired to manage had been dissolved, along with her job. This was both good and bad news. The positive side was that Edie could now provide full-time care for her mother. The negative aspect, however, was that Edie loved being a career woman. The money she made enabled her and Glenn to enjoy a debt-free life, and she received an immense amount of satisfaction by making a worthwhile contribution through her profession. Departing from her work life to care for her mother would mean she'd have to start over with her career at some point down the line. It would be a true act of love to sacrifice her career opportunities to do what was right. But Edie knew that she was choosing to stay at home not out of martyrdom or victimization. She had been raised to understand the importance of helping others, and what better example of that was there than to help her own mother?

By 2003, Harriet's health was rapidly declining. Edie became homebound virtually twenty-four hours a day. She spent years filled with half sleeping, listening to calls for help, bathing, feeding, and providing medical care. Her days and nights were no longer her own. By now, the depiction of the perfect daughter willing to sacrifice all for her mother without complaint was beginning to shatter. Edie was only human and had the same weaknesses that we all do. There were fleeting times when Edie was nearly overcome with frustration and grief. She watched as her siblings blissfully lived their lives, coming and going when they pleased, sharing stories of their seemingly carefree lives and vacations—their freedom. She heard from former business associates about their successes and longed to be among them. Her family's monthly income was cut in half with the added expenses for her mother. And there was no time for Edie to take a break from the daily routine to nurse her own aching physical health. She fought these tough times with courage, pep talks, and faith. In her rare spare moments, she tried to remember and experience the many gifts that God had given to the world and to her, struggling to get out of her self-pity and refocus on her mission and commitment. Prayer, the comfort of a loving and dedicated husband, and the love of her two sons, daughter-in-law, and grandchildren helped to ease her emotional bouts of depression, but a sense of aloneness still sometimes managed to drift in like a fog, enveloping her without warning or provocation.

The inevitable day came when Edie finally reached her limit. She did what she had vowed she'd never do: she and Glenn reluctantly admitted Harriet to the nursing home that Glenn managed. The guilt was overwhelming, but so was the challenge of caring for her. There seemed to be no other options. But as the weeks passed, Edie's guilt over their decision intensified. She watched as her mother defiantly resisted her new surroundings. Although she had some short-term memory loss with bouts of confusion and disorientation, Harriet was of sound enough mind to know that she was not where she wanted to be. No one was confused about her desire to vacate the place—immediately. After a few weeks of watching her mother decline steadily, Edie and Glenn brought her back home. This time, though, it was different. They hired someone to provide in-home care to assist Edie and give her some time to herself. It would prove to be a wise decision.

The guilt that Edie had been feeling, not only about the nursing home debacle but also about her fleeting pity parties for all that she'd given up, weighed upon her shoulders like a boulder. It wasn't until the hospice specialists came to help that Edie discovered she was not alone with those kinds of feelings. The specialists became the answer to her prayers. As Edie shared her innermost thoughts of guilt and failure, she learned that she was reacting normally to an exceptionally difficult situation. And as Edie turned over some of her daily chores and gained some quiet time to herself, she realized she had been completely burned out from the stress she'd been living with every day for so many years. As the days turned into weeks, Edie's strength and sense of well-being returned, as did her "can do" spirit.

On April 8, 2006, Harriet passed away with Edie, Glenn, and Edie's sons, grandsons, and oldest granddaughter at her bedside. The loss was immeasurable after Harriet's ninety-four years of life. She left behind the lesson to her children, her church, and the community that lasting happiness and joy comes simply from doing what's right. Edie is at peace with the knowledge that she did the right thing for herself. She was there for her mother when Harriet needed her most. And the rewards were far greater than any job opportunity or promotion could ever have been.

Now Edie is starting over. She is taking her talents and continuing to live according to the teachings her father taught her so many decades ago: life and happiness is about service to God through service to others. There is not a shadow of a doubt that Edie has honored her father's legacy. Her sacrifices were temporary, but her love and its memory will last a lifetime.

🌿   🌿   🌿

Author's Observations:

Edie's is truly a love story about unconditional devotion, acceptance, and sacrifice. Her loyalty to her aging mother, while putting her own desires and career objectives on hold, was an easy decision for her to make, but not always an easy one to abide by. There were lonely and worrisome days, sleepless nights, and times when she wondered if she could muster up the courage to go on. But the love and support of her family and friends was always enough to give her the energy to keep going. She will now reestablish her career and live her life knowing that she was there for her mother, just as her mother had always been there for her. Edie's story is a reminder of how important it is to never feel entitled to love, but rather to give it freely so that it can be returned unconditionally.

Summary

Adversity strikes all of us at some point in our lives, more often than not when we least expect it to. The women in these stories are no different. They were initially ill-prepared for their challenges, but through faith and love, they found and cultivated every ounce of courage possible to press on. Drained of energy and emotional strength, these women discovered that their passion for their missions energized them, rather than causing them to hide and wait for the storm to pass.

As many of these women admitted, denial was their first reaction to their circumstances. It offered protection from the overwhelming nature of the events they were each experiencing. But eventually, denial led to acceptance. These women played the cards they were dealt, honed the skills they had, and acquired new skills that they needed to successfully navigate the unknown territory ahead. Sacrifices were made, commitments were kept, goals were set, opportunities were seized, fears were managed, comfort zones were expanded, and victimhood was abandoned. Furthermore, formal education and material possessions were never mentioned in any interview as offering any advantage in navigating adversity. The soft (life) skills required to succeed were non-academic, and having an abundance of possessions was never identified as important in their journeys. Instead, fulfillment and courage were the result of their faith and their relationships, which were rooted in genuine and unconditional love.

Since many of these women experienced difficult childhoods, they learned the lesson early on that life isn't fair—it simply is what it is. We can either rise to the occasion and make the best of it, or we can live a life filled with negative emotions, thoughts, and actions. Protecting or denying someone the privilege of achieving personal growth as a result of adversity is truly a disservice to them. Teaching others, especially our youth, to solve problems and make good decisions while respecting themselves and others, developing loving relationships, and spotting opportunities embedded in adversity is the greatest gift we can give to anyone.

Crisis, the Chinese say, is defined as both danger and opportunity. So too is it with adversity. Each of these women lit up when they finished telling their stories, their voices and facial expressions revealing the thrill of their victories. Their struggles, though at times torturous and heartbreaking, were worth the personal gain they each attained. Their self-esteem and self-respect was heightened as a result of their tenacious willingness to find a way through their challenges. The courage they didn't know they had served them well, and will continue to serve them throughout their lives in adversities yet to come—as well as in helping others navigate through their own difficulties.

And happiness…well, there would be no such thing if it weren't for adversities. If life were perfect, there'd be nothing to celebrate and nothing to embrace; each day would be exactly the same. There's no joy to be found in avoidance.

In closing, it has been an honor and a privilege to have these women share their stories with me—and now with you. For many it was a difficult experience to reveal themselves and their failures, but they believed that if you as readers could benefit, it was worth the exposure. They know you are no different than they are. You too have unknown depths of courage inside yourselves that you haven't even begun to tap into.

If they could do it, so can you. We will be rooting for your success and may you be blessed with faith, love, and an abundance of courage throughout your journeys.

About the Author

SUE MACKEY is the founder of The Mackey Group (TMG), a nationally recognized skill-based development firm. As an experienced business columnist, she has written for the Washington CEO Magazine, the Bellevue Journal American, and a number of prestigious law journals. Women Navigating Adversity is her first in a series of "navigating" books and workbooks. After years of lecturing and conducting workshops, Sue has met many unsung and unrecognized courageous female heroes, quietly making their way through a variety of adversities. While it's unlikely these women will go on to head corporations, they are the integral backbones of families worldwide. Sue wanted to tell their stories in an effort to let others know that they are not alone in their struggles, and that there is hope and opportunity within every adversity.

WOMEN

NAVIGATING ADVERSITY

THE COURAGE THEY DIDN'T KNOW THEY HAD

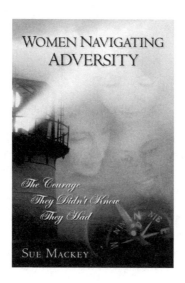

To order copies of Women Navigating Adversity
by Sue Mackey (Retail $18.95)

1 – 9	$15.00 ea.
10 – 24	$13.50 ea.
25 – 99	$12.00 ea.
100+	$11.00 ea.

Larger bulk quantity pricing available on request

Other books and workbooks brought to you by The Mackey Group

To order copies of *Living Well, Working Smart: Soft Skills for Success* (2005)
by Sue Mackey and Laura Tonkin (Retail $17.95)
1 – 9 $14.00 ea.
10 – 24 $12.50 ea.
25 – 99 $11.00 ea.
100+ $10.00 ea.
Larger bulk quantity pricing available on request

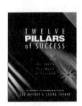

To order additional copies of *Twelve Pillars of Success Workbook*
by Sue Mackey and Laura Tonkin (Retail $12.95)
1 – 9 $9.00   ea.
10 – 24 $7.50   ea.
25 – 99 $6.00   ea.
100+ $5.00   ea
Larger bulk quantity pricing available on request

To order copies of *Twelve Pillars*
by Jim Rohn and Chris Widener (Retail $12.95)
1 – 9 $9.00   ea.
10 – 24 $7.50   ea.
25 – 99 $6.00   ea.
100+ $5.00   ea.
Larger bulk quantity pricing available on request

To order copies of *The Honey-Do Survival Guide*
by Sue Mackey and Laura Tonkin (Retail $15.00)
1 – 9 $11.00 ea.
10 – 24 $ 9.50 ea.
25 – 99 $ 8.00 ea.
100+ $ 7.00 ea.
Larger bulk quantity pricing available on request

Mail Orders:
The Mackey Group
PO Box 1247
Issaquah, WA 98027

Phone Orders: 425-391-8776

Email Orders: orders@mackeygroup.com

Standard Shipping & Handling

For Orders	Please Add
Up to $24.99	$4.95
$25 to $74.99	$5.95
$75 to $149.99	$6.95
$150 to $299.99	$8.95
$300 and Over	3%

Applies to US orders sent USPS Ground. Call for quotes on International and overnight shipping.

Title	Quantity	Unit Price	Total
		SUBTOTAL	
Washington residents please add 8.8% sales tax			
		Shipping	
		TOTAL	

Payment—please circle one: Check   VISA   MasterCard

Name:_____Phone: (_____)_____

Address:_____

City/State/Zip: _____

Email Address: _____

Credit Card Number:_____Expiration Date:_____

Signature:_____

For information about or to schedule a speaking engagement, please contact The Mackey Group at info@mackeygroup.com.